CAPTURED MOMENTS

Edited by Helen Davies

First published in Great Britain in 2012 by:
Forward Poetry
Remus House
Coltsfoot Drive
Peterborough
PE2 9BF
Telephone: 01733 890099
Website: www.forwardpoetry.co.uk

FOREWORD

In 2009, Poetry Rivals was launched. It was one of the biggest and most prestigious competitions ever held by Forward Poetry. Due to the popularity and success of this talent contest like no other, we have taken Poetry Rivals into 2012, where it has proven to be even bigger and better than previous years.

Poets of all ages and from all corners of the globe were invited to write a poem that showed true creative talent - a poem that would stand out from the rest.

We are proud to present the resulting anthology, an inspiring collection of verse carefully selected by our team of editors. Reflecting the vibrancy of the modern poetic world, it is brimming with imagination and diversity.

As well as encouraging creative expression, Poetry Rivals has also given writers a vital opportunity to showcase their work to the public, thus providing it with the wider audience it so richly deserves.

C🌐NTENTS

THE POEMS

THE YEAR

Back to the place where I first met you,
Standing there all shiny and new.
I remember every second as if it was yesterday,
Standing there awkwardly as you said hello,
Took my bag,
Then off we go,
The whole way there you couldn't take your eyes off me,
The whole way there I could hardly breathe,
Such an adventure for our first date,
Such a special person, I could hardly wait,
Who'd have thought this would be our fate,
To remain forever in this state.
Back to the place where I first met you,
To think of when I hardly knew,
There existed such a person as amazing as you.
The days go by oh so fast,
But somehow those first memories last,
Such a far cry from our lonely past.
Back to the place where I first met you,
Such a rapid change our life has been through,
I cannot believe that I found you.
Over seven billion people in the world today,
And I was lucky enough to find you in mine,
Our year together has been divine.
Like flying through space,
There's no time in place,
He put this smile upon my face.
No limits to this feeling of bliss,
And to think this all started with a kiss.

Amy Parkinson

A SEA BY ANY OTHER NAME

When it begins you're on the edge, a baby.
You dive into the liquid fire
Almost drowning in confusion.
You reach out, trying to find a shore.
Swimming, burning, holding onto nothing
Realising that's all there is.
Problems bobble on the surface
Before being lost like your own innocence.
A million swimming, burning souls
Around you going aimlessly in every direction.
Some diving down to the bottom
Looking endlessly for something
Others drown, not finding anything worth looking for.
Life is a fiery savage sea
Where human sharks bite and take.
They would say they need to survive.
But in the fire that is life's deep ocean
The truth burns everyone in their ponder.

John Ball

TED SHUTTLE

Ted you've the most loveable one,
Born the son of a snake catcher
You are the only one.
A multi-millionaire, a bear full of care,
A bear with no time to spare.
Constantly on the go
Different hats he wears through the days that go by.
Often he does his work and breathes a little sigh.
Upon a hammock in the afternoon he's found asleep,
So very sound.
Bees and butterflies flutter around
Birds sing a chorus, a magnificent sound.
Ted finally wakes; his day is done.
Stretches and looks at the setting sun.
Bumbles indoors for a cuppa and soon it's time for tea.
Goodnight Ted, God bless you.
Tomorrow is another day.

Joy Sharp

THE GUARDIAN

As a guardian of life,
The clock on the wall,
Records the time,
Allotted, to all.
We go thro' the day,
Living life, as we can,
With an eye on the clock,
Ever since time began!
Our days divided,
For work or play,
With hours for sleep,
At the end of the day!
Our lifespan is measured,
By numbers of years,
Which nothing can change,
Despite our tears
So, we take,
Each day as it comes,
To make our memories,
For all our young ones!
Maybe, when eons,
Of time, have gone by,
We will 'master' time,
To choose, when we die!
But until then,
The clock on the wall,
With relentless beat,
Controls time, for us all!

Evelyn Eagle

UNMOVED

Epic was the tale told
A story beginning to unfold
In it was a heart so cold
It froze the liquid molten gold

From within the darkest realms
A voice spoke of reason
Power erupted deep therein
And pleaded *rationality* . . .

Ghazal Choudhary

DANCE OF THE SACRED WHORE

. . . and within that sacred space
I call home,
I dance . . .
I dance with the universes,
galaxies, stars and solar systems . . .
I dance with black holes and white holes,
Portals of Energies . . .
and I dance with vacuums and vortexes
and through lights and darknesses . . .
through moons and suns
and with beings from neither here nor there . . .

And someday soon,
I shall dance for thee, my love,
dance in the dim shadows
of fluttering orange flames . . .
bare, brown and serpentine,
I shall dance for thee . . .
and as rare as my dark, Dravidian flesh is,
I shall dance and the Dance of Kali
for Thee . . . my love . . .
I shall dance the Dance of Kali . . .
for Thee . . .

Jacqueline Zacharias

FOR MY SCIENTIST FRIEND

Seek, no more my child
Come let us begin
This journey through life
My dear God speaks
Come unto me
Your spirit will rejoice
In the wisdom
Of His word
Throw away your
Doubts and fears
Your heavy heart
God loves you
With unconditional love.

Penelope Kirby

4

A POEM FOR MY SONS

This is all I have now, a photograph?
I was not there with you as I was left out!
All of the memories of when you were both young
Are all I have left of my two sons
Left and forgotten by one but he was not there.
Now the second, the youngest, is always close by
He came with me, my life to share.
I have loved you both and did what I could
But life has not always been so good!
There is no point in crying anymore
Or worrying when I will see my eldest
I cannot change the past, and
I cannot change his thinking!
I love them still and always will
And hope they will be happy.
But the days are short, and if he
Wants to see me
He will have to make it snappy
None of us know when we will go
It's in the hands of the Lord, you know.
Last moments, regrets and doubts, and wonder
Will be all that are left for you to ponder
Saying, 'I wish I had done this, or done that'
Will be empty words, too late, that's a fact!
So this little poem I have written to you both
Putting my feelings down is all I can do!
To let you know how much it hurts
When the ones you love are not there for you!
I wish you both all the happiness you can fulfil
From a mother who loved you and always will.

Miss Terry Thompson

YUMMY YUMMY

Yes, it's true, she used to be yummy,
But all that changed, when she became a mummy
Now it's dirt and diapers and sweating in the park
No longer yummy, and best eaten after dark.

Yvette Dawkins

LONDON OLYMPICS PRESS RELEASE

The London Olympics endeavours
To be diverse and inclusive, however
To achieve this we're making some changes
(Some minimal programme exchanges)

All poolside events will be dropped
In case those who can't swim throw a strop
We'll use the space as a place to relax
With soft drinks and delicious light snacks

There'll be something for all, we maintain
And lest our weight-watching patrons complain
We've agreed to lose synchronised swimming
And replace it with synchronised slimming

And then throwing the hammer must go
A complete waste of time as you know
But instead for the very mad-mooded
We reveal throwing a tantrum's included

Note – the ten thousand metres is out
It excluded all those who are stout
But there'll be fun for phenomenal eaters
So line up for the ten thousand pizzas

Our market research indicated
That generally sport's overrated
And that we'd rather not see florid faces
So we're axing the rest of the races

We've conducted our impact assessments
With the result we'll provide more refreshments
And our lawyers have sent confirmation
That with luck we'll avoid litigation

So no injuries, no broken bones
Just time spent with your families and phones
A triumph without legal claims
We present the Olympics without any games!

James Woolf

2004 COMMON RIDING DAY

Ghost lady of Langholm by chance we should meet
As I await the flute band in the High Street
You appeared, like an angel in the mist and the rain
One glace and you were gone. Will I see you again?
Or where did you go?
Will I see you again?

The following day when the rain turned to shine
You appeared again like an angel by the footbridge so fine
Your smile filled the air like the sweet aroma of flowers
That moment I knew I'd remember for hours
Oh where had you gone?

The band will play a sweet melody,
The beat of the drums brings you closer to me
With hair so fair, almost shining with gold
No one would believe in a story so bold
A story so bold.

As you emerge in the clearing, the sunlight does explode
From the dark treetops and onto the road.
In the distance your figure will fade in the haze
Oh beautiful lady, you'll always amaze
You'll always amaze.

Ghost lady, was it by chance that we met
On that misty morning both soaking wet?
(Yes, both soaking wet)
Over the heather and across the wee burn
Oh will you ever return?

I remember your eyes so dark and glowing
And your long dress that ever was flowing
It was a meeting that lives with me yet.
You're just a memory now.
A mirage, a meeting or was it a dream?
You never came back so I never knew,
Much of the old barley brew
(Well goodbye my lady)
Goodbye!

Brian Ritchie

RADIO VON

'Go on my son!'
Goes Von
To her nephew
Steph
When he stops
A ball in goal
Phew!
He wears Von out
She has to light up a fag
Red rag to a bull
Steph can't stop that!
But the breeze tries to fight her lighter
And is a friend
To her mum, dad and sister
Who wish lovely Von'd desist her
Her habit
'But the doc won't have it'
Von says sweetly
'He says cut down – don't stop completely
It'd be too stressful'
And if Von has to
She'll fight any chest infection
That could be a direction
On the treatment she receives
For a blip in her system
For which Von dons metal shoes
And turns clocks back
When she irradiates!

Wendy Young

WE SLOWLY FADE

In this world where we live
The joy of life slowly fades
The green grass around us
Slowly turns another shade.
Upon me is night and the end is in sight
God's grace be with me as I depart
Leaving a memory in my loved ones' hearts

Sally Fernee

8

I WONDER WHAT IT WOULD BE LIKE

I wonder what it would be like to be a shooting star
Would I persist or burn up before getting too far?
Just a streak across the sky and then be done
Or maybe I could provide a wish for everyone.

I wonder what it would be like to be the sun
Not to rain and snow on everyone.
Would my energy just shine, providing light?
Could I help a poor soul, escape from the night?

I wonder what it would be like to be the moon
If late at night I worried the sun would come soon.
I could see myself a million miles away
But no one would hear the words that I say.

I wonder what it would be like to be the sky
I would just be awesome, no one larger than I.
Would I remain humble or would it go to my head?
Although I am blue I can turn the sun red.

I wonder but realise I am just me
Kind of a collection of all things I see
I don't know the future or what shall be
I just know that the apple doesn't fall far from the tree.

Mark Russell

FAME?

What would it be like to be famous?
Known throughout the land!
My name on every tongue
Would it really be grand?
Now my mind goes quiet –
Fame wouldn't suit me –
Although I like making folk laugh,
Within – I'm shy – you see!
So, I won't seek stardom
Floodlights, success and fame.
Once you hit the headlines
Life can never be the same.

Barbara Buckley

CRIME

Moving house, a challenging time
Move in quickly and settle down
Think of everything, except of crime
Couldn't happen to me, not in this town
Go to bed and lock our door
Snuggle up, your eyes seek sleep
An opening door, your feet on the floor
A hooded shape, a silent creep
Suddenly a voice, loud and clear
'Get out of my house,' try not to weep
Disappearing shape, doors open wide
Hearing your heartbeat you try to peep
Can't believe it, it's gone outside
No sign, no time, never been found
A broken plant pot on the ground
After a time you start to live
Can you do it? Can you forgive?

Elizabeth Corr

WHIZZY JOJO

Whizzy JoJo doesn't shirk
There are rooms to clean
She's hard at work.
But in her eyes where laughter lurks
And around her mouth
Plays little smirks
Friends wonder what she's thinking of
Could it be? Is it love?
But Whizzy JoJo doesn't stop
Right now she's being Mrs Mopp
No diversion from the task
Her friends don't see the need to ask
About diversions and imaginings
And a smile that hints at other things.

Richard Hayter

NIAGARA STORY

Journey to Niagara in a black limousine
First a South African family,
Second a couple from Toronto
Third a couple from Vancouver
A long way from their birthplace Iran
Last person to join us a young man
Who was ½ Brazilian, ½ Japanese
Our own united nations
South Africa, Iran, Japan, Isle of Man,
Lots of miles we travelled
Passing through different towns
Shown what they had to offer – from
Wine growing/tasting, chiming flower clock.
Arrival in Niagara, welcomed by its roar
The awesome spectacle leaves you overawed,
The curtain of water thundering to the rocks
Donning our waterproof coveralls
We get onto 'Maid of the Mist' a sturdy craft
That takes us from the shore,
Taking up position standing at the rear
The exhilaration fills me as the first falls we pass
The large, leading to the Little Miss
A few yards yonder, just as exquisite
We sail into the main body
The mist is all enveloping, senses respond with excitement
Tightening the body expectantly
Cameras held tight, 'Don't let go!'
Or later you will miss the show
Disembarking, what a delight, senses all a-quiver
Instead of being over a lake, it was more a mighty river,
The final destination, walking thro' well-tended gardens
The sights that greet are almost too awesome to describe
Fast flowing river with the white horses – rushing to the edge
There its weight disgorges, the mist that rises displays
Before our eyes, the most beautiful 3D rainbow
Justice cannot be done by the photos taken
Voraciously enjoyed, taken home
Remembrance of all that we've enjoyed.

Elizabeth Adams

SAD, LONELY AND DOWN AND THE CAFE

Sometimes we get sad, lonely and depressed, So I suggest we put on our coats and go for a
walk and look around.
Take pressure from your mind and you feel refreshed.
You might meet a friend and there's a café down in town
Just a homely place if you are feeling down,
A cup of coffee or a good meal
A pleasant boy who talks
And fills you full of joy,
With his jokes and laughter,
Trying to give each and everyone,
Something they are trying to find,
A pair of blue eyes are full of honesty,
Those big brown eyes are full of loyalty,
And a shade of hazel eyes, are full of sincerity,
But when I see those green eyes,
They were full of envy and full of jealousy,
Perhaps it could come after,
And believe me, who knows when you are feeling down and feeling blue,
You could meet someone in this café who is honest and true.

William Deaves

O! THOSE SWEET, SWEET

Golden bells ringing in my ears
They tell me a tale that Christmas is here,
Those sweet chiming bells.
That tell me Christmas morn is here
Love, hope, happiness.
Those sweet chiming bells ringing in the town
So awake, awake they do say
Those sweet chiming bells
The Lord is here, come, come gather near
Come from afar those golden bells, bells that do ring
Come and worship the one is here so celebrate
Tell you now with those chiming bells
That ring so far and near
He says my love for you will always be here
Those sweet golden chiming bells, that ring in our ears.

Deborah Storey

THE MONKEY PUZZLE TREE

When this Monkey Puzzle Tree was growing,
Along where now the North Sea is flowing,
Some dinosaurs were roaming hereabout,
One of them, assailed by sudden doubt,
Asked, 'Why do Monkey Puzzle Trees grow here?
I have never seen one monkey appear.
It's too warm to run so I'll just amble.
By this tree, I'll just let my thoughts ramble.
The oddest notions flit through my head,
Mammal, Monkey, Man, when dinos are dead.
Monkey Puzzle Tree, keep on baffling me
. . . But you block thoughts of our posterity.
Monkey Puzzle Tree, I can see a cliff,
Within it are dinosaur bones – as if some dreaded
Disaster must befall us all.
Monkey Puzzle Tree, also your downfall
Though my fossilised bones may be found – yet
Monkey Puzzle Tree, you turn up as JET!

All this dinosaur had no wish to hear,
They scoffed that sunstroke must afflict their seer.

Christine Creedon

OCTOBER

O n All Saints' Eve
C omes Halloween,
T rick or treat
O n doorsteps.
B eware of witches
E xorcise ghosts
R elinquish all your demons.

Joyce Walker

FLORAL DELIGHTS

Mr Bee, buzzing by the window,
Saying good morning to us, you see,
Before he buzzes in the flowers,
Out in our garden, continuously,
The bluebells, so blue,
With perfume so heavenly,
Especially when the sun shines,
On other bells of pink and white, plus honesty,
The tulips red and gold, have opened to the sun,
When the sun goes in again,
They close up, one by one.
So many flowers to come,
New ones, soon to bloom,
Arranged some more, in flowerpots yesterday
To make themselves at home.
Flower catalogues are full of exotic blooms,
Wanting you to buy them all,
Maybe you will buy some
For your family and their homes,
Expensive they can be,
But what a garden you can make,
Of all those flowers, so heavenly.

Mabel Deb Moore

OLD HARRY

I was strolling down the lane
Early one evening in May
When I reached the bridge that place
Was where Harry the tramp did stay

He came up the bank in
His usual slow way
Then stopped for a word
About the weather that day.

When I reached home later that night
I happened to mention my meeting with Harry
'I am sure you did not,' my wife she did say
'For three weeks ago Old Harry passed away.'

Irene Barton

DID WE?

Sixty thousand,
God's gift to
Man. They
Gave their
Lives one day,
Just out of
The age of
Play.
Did we remember
Them or their
Families who say?
Who were they?
Pawns in the
Game of politics
Still goes on today.

Frank Oldfield

PREFACE

It beckons, sinister landscape of the deep,
Stygian aura of death and decay,
Vast submerged mountain chains,
Cavernous fissures of infinite gloom.

It thrums, subliminally in the ocean depths,
Regurgitation of the undisturbed.
The collective consciousness of life
Permeating the hermetic underworld.

The calling, of grotesque predators
Bathed in chemical ghosting light.
Trailing corkscrewed weapons of war
Or Pyrotechnic sniper scopes.

The signal, to venture into worlds unknown.
Perilous navigation to encounter;
Fraught with danger and hidden treasures,
So begins our adventure.

Chapter one . . .

Jill Pisani

DEAR MR PRIME MINISTERS

Regarding the national debt and the amount spent on overseas charity

I am no mathematician or politician
Nor so blind that I cannot see
The UK has debts in the billions
A figure too high for me to conceive

Now I'm not made of stone,
I feel for those who are poor
But shouldn't you first be helping,
Those close to your black steel door?

Billions of our hard-earned pounds,
You freely give away
While people like me are struggling,
For the food they eat to pay.

So why don't you ask the people
Whose money you give away,
What we really think
Let us have our say.

Some say we've a moral obligation
To give aid to every nation
I'm not looking for sympathy
But give my money back to me.

Tony Izzard

ECOLOGY EDICT

Gold, silver, gas, trees
Animals, plants, scientific disease
Man the enemy, Man the foe
Greed not need, results in woe
Take and take without redress
Our children inherit the inevitable mess
Stop the horror, stop the rot
This urgent battle must be fought
A perfect world, too much to ask
A better world should be our task.

Catherine Hislop

ORPHANS OF THE STORM

These two orphans of the storm.
Together in the Second World War.
Their parents killed during an air-raid.
Whilst they stayed the night with friends.
Now in the hours of grieving, separated.
Destined for separate county, orphanages,
Their pining for the other unbearable.
They corresponded by post weekly,
Which only emphasised their loss,
Finally they came together at sixteen,
As if released from sheer purgatory.
Their mutual affection overwhelming.
Their melting and melding inevitable.
The metropolis where they settled,
Such a nice, self-contained couple.
Lived in a small, utility bungalow.
A barrow boy and his cleaner wife.
She cleaned in a doctor's surgery.
All they sought was a good life,
Their relationship and their home,
Then along came a baby boy,
Quite normal – not genetically damned.
But an ordinary, delightfully cheerful lad.
To him they were just Mum and Dad.
Then at the council an officer blabbed.
From that the cat let out of the bag.
Are still the nice couple next door,
Alec sadly developed terminal cancer,
Alice took his painkillers willing
Lying together they died entwined.

John Pegg

THE ICE AGE

Into the glass the young man stared
And saw the world grow old
Before his very eyes the sun
Had suddenly grown cold

A darkness greater than the night
Plunged everything in gloom
And bitter cold came creeping in
The once familiar room

He looked again and dimly saw
The ocean's crumbled bed
Littered with a million wrecks
On which the urchins fed

Become a snow-white blanket now
As flakes began to fall
They settled on the broken earth
A shroud to cover all

Through the mist of frozen white
The young man saw no sign
Of living creatures on Earth
There was no trace or kind

The grip of ice had strangled
All that lived and grew
And brought the silence of the grave
To a world that never knew

The young man slowly turned away
So troubled was his soul
As he beheld an ice-cold world
Begin to spin and roll

Free of its orbit chains at last
It sped into the night
Onto its own destruction
A brilliant flash of light

Robert Stevens

WITH HAND ON HEART
(In honour of the lives lost in 9/11)

Like the phoenix that rose from the ashes,
High in the urban air,
New York in solidarity,
Has rebuilt what once stood bare.

By the edge of the Hudson River,
Under Manhattan's blue sky,
Stands proud the one World Trade Centre
That fills the sky on high.

A symbol of hope and resilience,
A symbol that fear has no part,
In a nation united in tragedy,
In a nation that touched the world's heart.

The pools of reflection beneath it,
Where the water does ever flow free,
Resembling the tears that have fallen,
For an attack on humanity.

The names of 3,000 remembered,
Inscribed in bronze, to endure,
Together in life, 10 years ago,
Reunited in death, once more.

A tribute to crews, who preserved life,
For the souls who were too young to die,
Take time to reflect and honour them,
May faith give you strength as you cry.

'Neath the stars and the stripes up above you,
Place your hand on your heart and show,
The pride in your nation, where peace has endured,
Where dignity and freedom do grow.

Immortalised forever,
Their names in our hearts will remain,
Where the pools of the water flow freely,
May your sweet memories sustain.

Sonia Limm

LOVE·HATE

I love you
I hate you
I never want to
Lose you

I want to kiss you
Caress you
Spend all my life
Beside you

I abhor you
I denounce you
I don't ever want to
See you

I shield you
And heal you
To prove that I am
True to you

I defy you
And reject you
I pitch myself
Against you

But through these times
No matter what
My heart bleeds only
Love for you

Love me
Hate me
Never ever
Leave me

Kiss me
Caress me
Spend all your life
Beside me

Abhor me
Denounce me
Don't ever want to
See me

Shield me
And heal me
To prove that you are
True to me

Defy me
And reject me
Pitch yourself
Against me

But through these times
No matter what
May your heart bleed only
Love for me

Christopher de Mercado

LOST CHILDREN

so anyway in this dream
I'm toiling away
in blistering heat
on a hillside in Palestine,
ploughing stony soil
with the jawbone of an ass
it's damned hard work
what with all the armed men
that keep leaping up out of the furrows
and the nasty little fragments of live scripture
this earth's infested with
they can suddenly blow at any time
causing heavy loss of life
I'm standing on the hillside gazing round
and in all directions, far as the eye can see
the phosphorescent glare
of flash new settlements:
well cities built on hilltops can't be hid
the Judean desert's all but gone
rough places straightened
the valley lifted up
exactly as promised
a six-lane highway scrawled across the plain
in the wilderness that's left behind
I wake up to the sound of many voices, crying

Andrew Greaves

THE DISEASE OF LIFE

All of us know at sometime or other
It might be an aunt, a father or mother –
The disease Alzheimer's is a name we fear
Because it could happen to someone who is near –
The signs at first are not very plain
Because the poor person is not in pain –
As time goes by the signs get worse
It's a pity we can't put Alzheimer's in reverse –
We visit the folk on a nice sunny day
They look at us but they have nothing to say –
Medical science is trying its best to resolve
Surely it's a must that we all get involved –
The folks themselves have their memories taken away
What have they left? Not even a special day –
We should to all of them make a fuss
And treat them only as one of us –
Don't forget they have birthdays, Christmas and times that are hard
So dip in your pockets and send them all a card –
Pay them a visit and take them out in the car
A ride in the country along pretty lanes but not very far –
Do your best for the time they are here
Then perhaps Alzheimer's we won't have to fear.

Eddie Owers

SPRING

The morn is bright
The sun is shining,
Across a clear blue sky
A hawk is flying,
The stream is flowing
Primroses smiling,
Hedgerows alive and breeding
Insects buzzing
Wildlife feeding
Trees dressing
Flowers awakening
Birds singing.
The countryside in spring . . .
New life beginning.

Arthur Pickles

THE FULLNESS OF TIME

Sculptured on the leaden grey sky tall gaunt branches spread
Naked, emaciated, shorn of adornment as the long gone dead
Winds harrowing painful joints stiffened by the cruel frost
Soon to be enfolded in a fleecy cloak safe from the wintery blast
As silently, softly, snowflakes flurry down and unfurl
Clothing in a pure white mantle the harshness of a barren winter world
Oh tree so regal in stately majesty, no longer drear and bare
Limbs now proudly encumbered reach out to the sharp clear air
Earth soon reborn discloses spears of colour and budding greens
Snickering, racing through vale and dell, a gay once slothful stream
The sun, long hidden, reaches out to every living thing
As sonorous strains of bird song herald the coming spring
Umbrella of green, now summer is high, appraise the earth so fair
Fledglings from the nest long gone soar free on the balmy air
Welcome shade, spread far and wide, succours the parched dry ground
Soon evening dew in light relief will everything surround
The days are growing shorter now as the fullness of time draws nigh
When our richly burdened, bounteous earth again in deep repose will lie
The pace of life confounding who of us pause to greet
Blandishments of nature or the seasons of our trees.

Doreen Goodway

YUKON'S MOON

Silhouette their tall
Wintry shapes,
Tinted in silver
Draped in firs
Majestic . . .
Deserts of snow,
Eternally the crystals
Dance and glow
By lunar light
Where famished green-eyed
Lupine lurks and rakes
In Yukon's wilderness.

Terrence St John

THE STORM

The sea is leaden grey,
Almost as heavy as,
The black thunderclouds,
That gather above me.
Sucking the moisture from the air
Bringing the swirling tempest.

Further to shore
I stand upon the beach
Sand amongst my toes,
Soaked shoes in hand
Just . . .

Watching as the fading light,
Bleaches the colour out of everything.
Black and white
Sharp electric light
Forking its way across the blackness
Ripping . . .

The sky apart.
I should go home
But I won't I'm not wanted there
But I . . .

I want this,
This moment,
To last forever.
For eternity
I feel the fear
Of the land . . .

Waiting
With baited, trembling breath
For the storm to
Strike.
I feel
The destructive rage of the sea
And the pain
Of the sky, as it's torn
Asunder
I'm part of this,
This . . .

Special communion
I hear the crash of the waves
The howling of the wind,

The shrill shriek of thunder, of lightning
'Look at me! Look at me!'
All around me is . . .

Evidence
Of the raw destructive force of
Nature of a power that also
Creates
A power we try to imitate,
Yet ultimately
Fail to . . .
Match.

Joscelyn Heath-Collins

DON'T BE FOOLED

Don't be fooled by what you see:
The steady breathing, quiet me,
Eyes shut, apparent peacefulness
Hiding inner-restlessness.
Lying, fearing what's ahead;
Light's darkness now I face with dread,
End of night, start of day . . .
I wish I was another way.

Unreal reality of dreams,
Coming to an end, it seems.
Force my eyes to see the day . . .
I wish there was another way.
The dark discomfort of my sleep
Envelops me, takes me deep
Into a place where I can hide,
I wish that I could stem this tide.

Of inner-turmoil, frightened me,
How she wants so much not to be
Fenced in by fearful hopefulness
With all the need of self-defence.
Oh how I wish I could be,
Not wild, but absolutely free
To run and see who I can be
If I can only just be *me*.

Val Bolam

MEMORIES OF DIANA

Us old folk we fear not death,
As we await the day with bated breath,
And when the time comes for us to die,
We'll meet again our Lady Di,
She'll hold our hands and calm our fears,
We will still be brushing away the tears,
Let's think of Di, at Christmas in the simplest of ways,
And all the good she did for us, sadly in too few days,
Of all those ailing hands she held,
To bring some sort of hope,
And all of us in need of love,
She showed us how to cope,
Di was a bright and shining light,
That helped us on our way,
But that light dimmed one August night,
And simply slipped away,
To have lived our lives in the same lifetime,
As that girl with face so fair,
Was a bonus for us ordinary folk,
Just to breathe the very same air.

Fred Wallis

ALL YEAR ROUND - HAIKUS

Winter's low weak sun
Coldest season is to come
Snow dusting, good fun

Blossom's flowering
Spring leaping, bounding, bouncing
Raindrops showering

Day sky full of zest
Summer sun no time to rest
Baby birds leave nests

Autumn leaves falling
Meandering breeze snaking
Wind trees exposing.

Margaret Harris

SING TO ME

Sing to me sweet siren
Lay me in your arms
Let me stay beside you
And hear the beating
Of your heart.
Sing to me of princesses
Locked in ivory towers
Sing to me of love
And all the beauty it inspires.
Sing to me of knights,
So brave, so noble and true
Sing to me of fairy tales,
And forgotten lands of old.
Softly hold me to you
And warm me with your breath
Keep all I fear at bay
And forever keep me safe.
Sing to me sweet angel
As I lie with you tonight,
Sing to me so softly
And kiss me through the night.
Sing to my lover
Sing unto my heart,
Sing your beautiful love song
And say we'll never part.

Melissa Buhagiar

A BLACK AND WHITE PHOTOGRAPH

The photograph was of a scene,
Of dark and light and shades between.
Twisted shapes and bulbous mounds,
Between the skyline and the ground.
As the imagination caught the spark,
Of light, penetrating the dark.
Great monsters grew and beings were strangled
Among the branches all entangled.

Elizabeth Fleischer

EMPTY CITY

Loneliness bought and loneliness sold
Exploiting the young fresh from the fold
Old men with wine, paupers within
Bag lady shuffles out in the cold

Breathing in carbon, light up a fag
Destitute, scruffy, he begs for a drag
Cardboard for shelter, a life in a bag
Hollow eyes just empty and dead

People rush by, cars now collide
Mother and baby, young girl at her side
One's chasing rainbows, one's in the road
Beggar man, thieves and one stolen bag

Carrying burdens like hearts on a sleeve
As one woman faints another does sneeze
Picking up dog ends, picking up crabs
The one on the corner, she's up for grabs

Selling their methadone, selling their soul,
Discriminating not the young or the old
Chasing the dragon, tightening grip
A ten pound bag for the mainline hit

Hiding in shadows then scurry away
Ten floors above the suits and well paid
Corporate towers proclaiming their wealth
Down in the gutter someone needs help

Top shelf material struts with her bags
M&S, Top Shop, Miss Selfridge or Next
Coffee at Costa, Starbucks or home
Dinner and cocktails, the party at eight

A scream with a shout then someone's laid out
Blood on the pavement, new training shoes
Off in the crowd to hide out of sight
One miserable bastard can't get a light

Rats from the sewer emerge for the night
At home with the revellers ready to fight
Calling for taxis, eating kebabs
Screwing in doorways, ex-servicemen brag

Spunk down an alley, they puke in the street
One man unconscious, there's blood on your feet
Girls are now fighting, letting it loose
Torn skirts and false nails, one a lost tooth

Vicious boys with their trophy girls
High on their arm and all tits and curls
Designer jeans for designer names
Displaying behaviour on their streets of shame

A pizza or slice, curry with rice
Asleep in the doorway, the one with head lice
Checking you out, wouldn't think twice
Of rolling you over for the price of a pint

The stench of stale piss, one defecates
Discarded tampons pulled out in haste
Animals loose from inside a zoo
Roaming the night with the homeless queue

Rubbish left randomly, condoms and pants
Blown to the gills where the misfit rants
Preaching of sins and finding his solace
From a bottle of sherry full of false promise

Some make it home, they long for a bed
Covered in blood or just a sore head
The dogs they come home, the cats they go out
A wife gets a smack, punch or kicked out

A city in slumber, tramps in a skip
Cold feet for breakfast, the first morning nip
Road sweeper hums keeping it neat
Treading the beat of a thousand feet

New sun arrives, the dust blows away
Ready for action, work, rest and play
Repeating its order night after day
The way of the city pulls us astray

Chasing the money or chasing a fix
Workers at work, young girls on the street
Regular johns, pickpockets, thieves
Rushing around to fulfil their needs

Shopping or browsing, take in the view
Or low life and high life, a mixed human stew
Doorways and dustbins, fashion and grace
You'll find it all in this cold empty place.

Paul Nicholson

GAME OF LIFE

He wins every time
Like a game of chess
I don't know the rules
Now, if it were Cluedo
I'd know who done it
I'd have ticked my boxes
Moved my piece
Asked all the right questions
Got the right answers
This is not Cluedo.

He wins every time
Like a game of chess
I don't know the rules
Now, if it were Monopoly
I'd have counted my money
Shared it among my properties
Passed 'Go', collected some dosh
I'd have gone to jail
I'd know why I was there
This is not Monopoly.

Every time
Like a game of chess
I don't know the rules
Now, if it were Snap
I'd place down my card
Wait for one the same
Share a likeness of sorts
Yell and reach for the same
I know I'd gathered it correctly
This is not Snap.

He accuses.
He sentences.
He makes his move,
Taking down all my defences
A pawn, a rook, a knight
Then he spins the board.
I think I've won,
He spins the board again and jumps,
I've lost
This is his game with my life.

Leigh Wolfe

UNCOMFORTABLY NUMB

To say the loneliness I feel in my soul
Has torn asunder
The majestic warmth of this
savage garden's wonder,
Is to have some sort of honesty
Uncomfortably numb
And a panicking connection
At least to some.

Weathered courage of some conviction
Not always valiant,
Through Alice's looking glass
The cracks apparent.
To find some bittersweet release
I go to the stable
The repeated mistakes
Of the horse at the table

They say the joker put a smile on that face
Once more with feeling
And gladly follow the wheelers
No time for healing
And so these awkward words of mine
My fable they try to sell
Through a tempest of abandonment
Perhaps the reason I fell.

Andrew Quick

LIFE
(To G Hempel)

My sea is empty, and so is my sky,
The sun blinds eyes, resting on a field of rye.
My blood forms mazy scarlet patterns,
The past drains wells of sparkling lanterns.
A sudden fall of rain washes off my face, crushing memories,
Voices are hushed by the drops of harmonies.
A wave of life sweeps away my time,
And I am shouting on a beach of dreams, not caring a dime.
The sea hides traces of my feet and life does wreathe,
Warming heart, making it eager and hard to breathe.

Roman Mikhalyuk

IN THE FLESH

He left the smell
Of his skin
On the sheets,
Mixed with sweat and blood;
And love,
He left her with a glance
In a frame.

Fled.
He fled.
Her flesh and blood frightened him;
And flash.

The day was nice
For some;
But she,
A shame covered
Her moaning.

Running.
He is bristling like a cat
And fear of the unknown
Is husking his sore throat.
He cannot forget.

She cannot forget.

A gentle way he was taking
Her virginity away.

He is in the flesh,
But very dead for the girl
With a shrivel feeling in her womb.

Ljubica Trninic

LET GO

You used me and abused me
Cos you were scared of what might happen
If you let go
Let go
You turned me away
Broken heart and broken-minded
You never meant to hurt me
You said
So many things going through my head
You pushed me out
And then I ran
Straight to the arms of another man
Starting to feel myself let go
Now I see you,
Telling me he's no good
He can't love me the way he should
Do you think you could love me better?
Guess we'll never know
Because you just can't let go
Let go
You left me broken-hearted and shattered
The pieces were scattered
I picked them up
And started again
And you're too late
Cos I have moved on
Your chance passed by
And now it's gone (gone, gone)
And I have let go.

Lucy Dowding

HI STREET

Browns, blues, greys and shades.
Pixie, bobs and long locks
Tousled bed heads and caps.

Leopard, floral, top buttoned-up
Boundaries blur for the metro age.
Fuchsia nails tap at iPhones.

The liberal beside me cynical of the scene,
The concrete catwalk.
Maskless, some drown in the town.

Coffee shops, fag stops, Big Issue sellers
Walk the path paved with gum stains.
Foot pains, shoes scream on shop floors.

Thread frays like the shoppers' days,
Closing time dawns on them that
The perfect top is yet to be found.

Don't fret, you can shop on the net.

Jenn Hart

LONDON ON MY MIND

I had a dream about rain last night,
London came into mind,
After class, walking in the rain in my rainy boots,
Books and lectures during the week,
Long walks and sun in the weekends,
Museums, coffee shops, bookstores,
I was alone yet I was with the world,
Trafalgar Square, Covent Garden, Sloane Square,
First day at a job and I have nothing to wear!
Bloomsbury, Kensington, Notting Hill,
Those streets come with a lyric in the back of my head,
'Runaway with my heart'
That is what The Calling said,
Love Actually around me and on screen,
These legs have taken me everywhere,
In the busy streets of London.

Metaxia Tzimouli

REMINDERS OF THE TIME

Final chimes of the old year sound
Reminders of the time –
Twelve months again now hastily passed,
Maybe New Year brings at last
Chances to make fresh peace.

Journey's end of all that's gone,
Reminders of the time –
Memories linger on what has been,
Images held of all that's been seen
As days have sped along.

There goes another year of life,
Reminders of the time –
What has gone cannot be restored,
Whether life was wasted by word or sword.
Time for renewal of peace.

Year's end is near, soon will be done –
Reminder that life goes on –
Put aside squabbles, make a fresh start,
Find a stillness in the heart,
Year's end brings in the new.

Ann Voaden

TO OUR CHILDREN

We pray you find in nature's path your sacred place,
Your gilded bough, the golden daisies' blazoned branch,
Blue, cloudless skies for your cathedral's base,
Your tempting music, echoing to entrance.

For incense burning on the fire that glorifies the air,
Once tired, the grass turf for a bed –
The earth which replicates a glade,
The stars a canopy instead.

We pray that you will love the things we love –
The ferns that greet, though wet with dew;
When rising, the sun, his shimmering rays will play,
In virgin forest where you choose to view.

Nola Small

GROWL

The body, this body, this body is a house of rumbling mutters
Like clapped thunder about to crumple;
Floorboards rip, roar, explode, collapse,
Revealing a kid angel with venom wings mumbling mercies;
Mercy on my hands, my eyes, my thoughts, everything that remains

Of this house,
This body, this weapon's no good –
Merely a gravestone begging for a living cyclone.
The voice is a wandering tombstone wrapped in meteor bones,
A catapulted tornado claiming the tailwind motion of breath,
A gale force land-locked and hurricaned. In the eye of the storm

I realise: life has something more to offer; and that steady unsteadying pulse
In your bloodstream, ribcage, display of breath
Tells me there exists stillness between each ravaging inhale and exhale;
Still like a ghost who never whispered his last words: 'There is something coming.
There is. And I feel it. Something is coming.'

A voice piercing silences,
Pounding static like air wishes it could:
Like Zeus meeting Quetzalcoatl in a cockfight;
Beating one another outside beauty, brilliant even,
In a wake of their own destruction. My tongue
Compresses feeling and sound into carbon diamonds,
Into lightning storms, crackling spirit and momentum
Back into words, one sound calling on angels of desolation.

Speaking only remorse and redemption, I let go
And I surrender, leaving breathing and space,
Half the temptation to create
Evil or knowledge –
I growl at the un-mutable future of perpetual presents,
The unending reverb of human-facilitated degradations,
Refusing to believe in the rampant polarisation of life,
Until that moment of revolution in which cycles are not magnets

But hold your breath –

They are tugging; this pulling is a burden without reprieve.
Human will has no melting point.
Every capacity for atrocity remains, existing,
Pulsing like blood in a vein that will never run dry.
There are some things we simply can never imagine.
Evil and good
Working counter-clockwise and calculated in a yin-yang periphery of honesty;

Honesty; this future is still a choice,
Is dust settling on bodies we haven't used properly.
Our voices are as still as the dust gathering,
This voice does not whimper;
But this voice cannot howl:
This voice only growls.

Growls at the smallness of its release,
Growls for what we dream to be –
Maybe one day reach –
Every capacity for creation existing beautifully;
Like a chrysalis in any season we choose,
In moonlight always, a cherry blossom made of snow and blood,
A music note wrapped in gold ribbon and autumn leaves,
The amber lens of a telescope facing backwards
Confirming the forward future brilliance of the human body:
Of motion, sound, and dust; harmonious and lifting.

Kevin Hageman

GODS AND MORTALS

Gods and mortals . . . unite as in a dance!
You see! There really is no difference
Gods on high are mounted on winged horses
A mortal falls – who whipped his horse to prance
Gods laugh and say . . . 'Were horses meant to dance?'
Gods reign on high and sip the golden wine
Mortals get high, and feel they are divine,
When gods look down and see a mortal's fate,
They smile and simply say in some defence,
That mortal must have died for love or hate
And comes to us to learn the difference.
Gods and mortals unite as in a dance!
And teach us how to use our common sense
To prove there really is no difference.

Valerie Hall

SHELTER

(To Anita)

In his times of tempest,
   A wave.
   An arrow
       Pierced the stone.
A book, three pens – one black, one red, one green –
         Drew on his chest the door, a country.

Where the winds
        Wail and
        Shred the shores
An arrow, a blade
     Slashed her flesh, carved a space.
A book, three pens – one black, one red, one green –
        Sketched on her back a map, a plan.

Where the winds
        Ravage the rocks
They carved and
    Opened   Themselves to each other,
    Enveloped   One another.

With their flames of red moisture
    They melted their mirrors,
    They built a ball of time.

        They filled it
       With their warmth,
        Their plans
         – flights and laughter and mutual exploration,
        Their maps
         – their gulfs, valleys and dunes,
        Their kisses
         – deep and alive, they were the spring, tobacco and wine,
        Their laughter
         – their light and their warmth.

        Their dictionaries
         Which, in their multitudes, couldn't contain
             Themselves, each other.

Gustavo Arevalo Rendall

EVERYTHING WE ARE

Everything we are
A twinkling star trying to be great
So many mistakes take their toll on my heart and soul,
My heightened resolve, everything we are
A higher faith, everything we are,
The destinies we shape,
Even though we find it hard, trying to awake
No longer mentally and physically scarred,
But my resolve will never break,
Everything we are, the hardships that we face . . .
My heart races, a further embrace . . .
Than the stars . . .
In space, marred through hardships . . . and hate
Trying to escape to a private place
Lift from the frustrations in my wake . . .
The heartache . . . maims, barely awake.
Who we are makes us what we are . . .
If that's the case . . .
Truth is never too far.

Brian Hewerdine

TROUBLE AND STRIFE

My bed is a mess
My body is making sounds.
I can get away with carelessness. You're no longer around to see.
And it's too late now to apologise.
You can't ignore the words.
I wish you'd seen my face when I knew I'd done my worst.

Actions speak the loudest, no matter how loud we scream.
And the one who stands the proudest beats the one who makes the scene.

Calm down, don't go, I'm sorry.
I was wrong, swept along in a rage.
Please wait, slow down, so sorry.
Turn the leaf, turn the cheek, turn the page.

Turn around and face me.
It's not that hard to do.

Easier said than done, when it's me hurting you . . .
I'd be walking away, too.

Katy Osborne

REBORN

Another moon died,
And was reborn in the sky.
Another sun rose
And went with the dark.
Another day arrived
And replaced the one gone by.

Another fire was lit,
And the room became warm.
Another rain calmed,
And then rose the rainbow.
Another door closed,
And opened the new.

Another man suffered,
And the other laughed.
Another tear dried,
And then smile awoke.
Another silence came,
And vanished the words.

Another truth was said,
And destroyed the lies.
Another challenge was won,
And a man's strength was grown.
Another world vanished,
And the new one was born.

Gita Liepa

THE FLU

Inanimate objects became animated as you sneeze loudly
Alone at home: you lie on the settee, pump up a cushion
For your head to rest:
It falls to the floor,
It lands on the green carpet,
You bang your head!
The television remote control slips out of your right hand
With the flu, inanimate objects, become animated.

Edmund Mooney

CHRISTMAS LAST!

This year Christmas came early and went.
Now I've to pay back what's been spent.
There's a credit card bill that's arrived on the mat.
It can't possibly be as much as that!

Can it? I can't pay all that back in one go
So I'll have to pay interest. Oh no!
So Christmas now's lost all its interest
And there's no time for me to 'ave a rest

Before Christmas comes again next year,
(God forbid it's in June, my dear!)
But if Christmas is gone, in the event,
And as yet I've to still pay the rent

Why's my house full of tinsel and bling?
With everyone doing their own thing?
And the bell on the church going *bing-bong!*
And we're all still singing a carol song?

Last year I had Christmas in March
'nd Chrissy decs led a merry dance.
The tree by then had gone nude
(The fairy on top thought it quite rude!)

Pine needles on carpet knee-deep!
Vacuum cleaner bust in a heap,
No sales around to get one cheap,
Their price today is very steep!

My pension won't go that far
At this rate I'll have hysteria
'nd fall in a heap on the floor
Or maybe run out through the door

And paint the town pillar-box red
As if I've gone off my head!
I probably have to boot
But really I don't give a hoot!

So when will be Christmas next year?
It will change again I fear.
Will it be in May or November?
I only hope I'm able to remember.

Jean Ivatt

DEAR FRIEND, I WORRY THAT IF I LEAVE YOU

Dear Friend,
I worry that if I leave you,
I will never see you again,
If you don't come to visit me,
I will understand.
My trip is quite a distance away,
And I am afraid when I return,
I won't see you.
My eyes drop tears,
If I return, brother, what will I find?
It I return and see you once more,
I speak to my heart,
As I move away from you,
And to it say amazed,
How could I ever leave you?
The village we grew up in, is rubble and dust,
Only the old people are left here.
The smoke and cries are still lingering here.
Your loss brings me sorrow,
And I am afraid when I return,
I won't see you.

Aqeel Ali

JUST DOING OUR JOB

I drive around the area in my bin wagon, doing my best with all of the slagging.
Move the stupid thing cos I can't get bloody through, if you don't move it then I'll report you.
I'm really, really sorry friend, I've got a job to do, report me if you want to it's entirely up to you,
I'm trying my best, it's a thankless task, driving around with a happy mask,
Why do you hate me and what would you do, if I were not there working for you?
Who takes your rubbish and keeps your streets clean, me and my lads do . . . so why be so mean?

Peter Elstob

MY LIFE

Mind troubled; cannot speak,
Disturbed nights make me weak.
Worries go round and round,
Long to move underground.
'It'll be fine,' my friends say!
Live my life for a day?

Then some empathy I would receive,
Friends would change thoughts on what they perceive.

Lonely – piece of my past,
I'd enjoy life at last.
Laugh loud with happiness,
But, no escape I guess?

Susan Mullinger

REMEMBRANCE

I remember the snowdrops in the snow
And the sound of bluebells in the woods.
I remember the cries of the newborn lambs
And the ravens black against the clouds.
I remember the plovers on the ground
And the swallows flying all around.
I remember the owls in the churchyard high
And galloping stallions by and by.
I remember the storms hitting the ground
And the cunning fox outwitting the hounds.
I remember the billowing wind in the trees
And the seagulls inland from the sheltering seas.
I remember the otters in the streams
And my grandfather and his dying dreams.
I remember the badgers in their sett
I remember them all; I won't ever forget.

Geoffrey Kendall

AN ALTERNATIVE CHRISTMAS

With pencil poised, his thoughts amok
Unheeding eyes upon the clock,
He dreamed of trains and all things fast, of signal boxes and at last
His mum had said – 'Well, write it down,
Just make a note and don't forget Ben's sailing boat,
And Hesta's crib and doll with bib – she's only three – you see,
And Grandpa's scarf for when he's cold, we must take care, he's getting old.'
He licked the lead and tentatively began to spell
A train for me, a scarf for Gramps, a signal box – perhaps some lamps?
A boat for Ben to sail to sea, a doll for Hesta, she's only three.
How d'you spell kite, with lots of string?
Dad said that would be the very thing to have hung up in his stocking.
His eyes were glazed, his dream afloat, no one heard that ominous note,
That ominous hum, that drone – that drear that normally would hold such fear
Of things that fly by night or day, the things you wish would go away
No one heard.
The night has gone, the shadows past Christmas Day is here at last.
The sun shines on the glistening snow, on footprints running to and fro,
The sound of voices seems to grate the sad despair – 'We are too late'
The eerie calmness settles down on the little house at the edge of town,
A scarf flies sadly – a kite flies free – a crumpled doll lies in a tree
For Hesta – she was only three.

June Johnson

QUEEN-IN-WAITING

When first you step along that special path,
Aware you are much envied and admired,
A Queen in prospect, wearing ribboned – 'Bath',
Eventually – astounding when attired,
And knowing that of all such Berkshire maids,
You now have in your future certainly,
A name we will recall with little aids.
Whose date themselves provision royalty,
Bestowing that enchantment still to be,
Profoundly recognised, intensely known,
Preferred by those who crave stability,
And therefore wishing 'monarchs' on the throne:
Queen Catherine-in-waiting from afar,
May you be blessed and prove yourself our star.

Anthony Russell

REMEMBERING MY BABY BOY

You went like a shadow in the night
Born before your time
Although my heart still longs for you
I know that you're still mine
I see you in a land of sunshine
Both arms full of flowers
Laughing and playing happily
Among the golden showers
I still can see your little face
Your hair like softest gold
I know I can't forget you
Although I've grown so old
You'll grow in Heaven big and strong
And when the time is right
I'll come and hold you close to me
Like a shadow in the night.

Maureen Baxter

SOUTHERN JUNCTIONS

Oh the lonely junction, Seaton
(Closure – Beeching can be blamed)
Silent platforms – weather beaten
Rampant nature has reclaimed.

In the Fifties, crowds descending
Flocking to Jurassic Coast
Miles of beaches – never-ending
'Sunny' was a luring boast.

Waiting – Sidmouth branch connections
Passengers now congregate
Trains with those divided sections
Down from London running late.

Vanished – people clutching cases
Alighting at abandoned Chard
All these stations woeful bases
Remembered sadly by the Bard.

Steve Glason

A SUITCASE ON SKID ROW

It's time I was hitting the road
Just got to grab one thing and go
My battered old leather suitcase
A comfort for me on Skid Row

Steering away from the cities
Driving the dusty dirt back roads
I eat out of fast food diners
And sleep in derelict abodes

Sometimes I stay in cheap motels
One needs a little luxury
Bed, shower, shave, cable TV
Jack Daniel's keeps me company

I've be a fugitive for years
No family, no friends, no home
On my head was placed a bounty
Relatively relaxed I roam

But I should be hitting the road
Just got to grab one thing and go
My old suitcase stuffed with millions
A comfort for me on Skid Row.

Keith Miller

FIRST LOVE

Sometimes we please others, before we please ourselves.
Sometimes we give up our hopes, so they can have their dreams.
Sometimes we love others first, before we can love ourselves.
We put our lives on hold in order for others to live theirs.
We think more about the words we say to others, than the emotions
And actions we carry for ourselves.
No matter where we go in the world,
People we love dearest will always be our first love.
Family and friends we adore will come first,
No matter how hard we try.
Because they will always feel our first love.

Vanessa Henderson

SENSES

Have you ever thought
What a beautiful gift your senses are?
The eyes, in which you take a snapshot of
A moment that stays with you, forever in life.
The ears, through which you hear,
Spoken words of love or admiration.
The laugh of your friends,
And the feelings of people spread through sound.
The smell, of fresh flowers
Growing in the ground.
Tasting, a texture within your palate
Filling the emptiness of your stomach,
Melting your hunger away.
Touch, feeling the softness
Of warm sand beneath your feet,
The type that's hot to walk on in the heat.
All these are an essential part of life,
Whether evolved genetically
Or an act of Christ.

Emma Gardner

THE MINSTREL

Standing alone under the spotlight
Fingers caressing the strings
Of his instrument softly.
Words floating from between
His lips moist with tears
Running down his cheeks.
Words of love, words of longing
Regret and joy all in song
Lost in his mind
Paying no heed
To his audience
Imagination wandering.
Alone he stands
Bathed in limelight
Exposed for all to see
The minstrel performs.

Andrew McIntyre

I SHALL, I WILL

I'll shadow you, when it's dark or light,
When I have to, I'm prepared to fight,
If there's a chance, I will try,
I will grit my teeth, until I cry,
If I cannot walk, I will crawl,
If I cannot jump, I shall fall,
If he breaks a leg, or loses a limb,
Without a doubt, I'll carry him,
I can't give up, or lose my way,
I shall not sleep, night or day,
If I cannot follow, I will lead,
I will not die, I'll only bleed,
I'll breathe my last breath and scream my last word,
I must make sure, that I am heard,
I'll fight for you, until my demise,
When my mind is lost, and my body dies,
I will be there, when you can't go on,
When all is lost, and hope is gone,
I will comfort you until you cry no more,
And help you remember what you're fighting for.

Charlotte Beaumont-McAllen

THE GRADUATE

To achieve a 2:1 I had passion,
To succeed in what I set out to do,
I have developed determination,
To work under pressure and see things through,
I find different ways to challenge myself,
Keen, with a ready sense of adventure,
I refuse to remain sat on the shelf,
So, discover new places to venture!
I have a creative approach to tasks,
With built resilience, I can bounce back,
Disengaging from myself I wear masks,
With humour that I appear not to lack,
I love to engage through voice, song and art,
I'm bubby and ready to make a start!

Suzanne Oke

UPON VISITING THE WOLF OF BADENOCH'S TOMB

To the ancient Celtic seat in midst of winter's chill I went
To stand among the mist-draped monoliths
The frosted grass and hardened earth, a glaze.
Of diamonds scattered on the ground,
The sun, it wreathed a lonely figure in shadow
Caught cold upon its brilliant gaze.
Within these walls a wolf sleeps in armour,
One hand pressed against his princely chest
And thus his battles are over, his bloodlust slaked.
His eyes stare hard and defiant as when Elgin burned,
In life, a cruel and twisted tale of woe.
In death heroic effigy awaits.
I stood with reverence in my heart,
For a celebrity of a distant age where vicious deeds,
Wrought purity upon a wasted soul.
Alexander! He does not know of his renown,
His image proud and pious hides
A twisted heart as back as coal.

Richard Connor

UNTITLED

On the shelf they both sit,
The two of them so chick,
So tiny are these two friends,
Arms around each other they blend,

Their dress so smart and colourful,
Hair combed back and so black,
She is such a pretty girl
He the man so strong and bold.

On a pedestal these friends stand,
These two lovable tiny friends
So my friends to you I say,
Stay close to your family each day.

(Brother and sister is who we are)

Dilip Hallam

THE FIRST LOVE

When first a man looked first upon a woman
She was, to him, as beautiful as the moon.
Gazing at her; tender, strong and savage,
He longed to drown in kisses, like monsoons.

To sweep away the ground beneath his feet
And make her his new earth, his root, his soil,
His cradle in his springtime second birth.
Like autumn leaves, though dying she'd not spoil.

And, like me, she'd all the shades of light;
What need had he for shapeless, bloodless skies
When he could track the constellations in her dreams
And trace the swallow's valour in her eyes?

And, naked, she approached him, naked as birth
And innocent and shameless, open, bare,
Still streaked with dirt from Nature's waking kiss
And leaves and insects twining in her hair.

With fierce new ardour, fair like I could feel,
He yearned to be the oak leaf knotted through,
To voyage in the jungles of her hair,
Lost by all but she, who he could never lose.

Between them he could see with sailor's eyes
A maelstrom to dare or drown his heart,
Then strange and wild country, rich new world,
Him calling to discover, every part.

That haunted shore that beckoned him to journey;
Like I might, in my distance being alone;
Where he would learn new spins in circle seasons
And in unconquered furrows rest his home.

Snow-silent both, they wandered long past dusk,
When shadows marked the contours of her form,
That foreign form embraced by secret dark,
Awakening in him a thrilling summer storm.

He took her hands, the human hands, like his,
And kissed the lips, the cheeks, the eyelid's crease
And all of perfect Eden turned to her;
The earth her skin and fevered pulse beneath.

The wind became her breath, her sighing oaths,
And sugar scents of vine-rose laced her skin,
The hearts of Eden pounded in her kiss,
The pounding hearts of lovers born as twins.

She slept upon his breast, he watched her face
And saw the swirl of nebulas and galaxies,
The deep eternity of space, and felt
The endless thread that ravels gravity.

They loved the love, the first love, first of all,
With only two on Earth, what eyes could pry?
Convention lost in lands devoid of time,
Before the crowding hours asking *why?*

And, walking through the world those lovers built
When love was all they had for clay and bricks,
I glimpse odd petals drift from paradise,
Like sunlight in the hill-mist playing tricks.

And each one in my soul is pressed and watered;
The plain can hope, and in that hope believe
That in me is the love to plant another Eden,
If love can make me another Adam's Eve.

Holly Bee

AN AFTERNOON WELL SPENT

I called in at a garden centre just the other day
I only stopped to look around and pass an hour away
Oh the glory of the colours, the blues, the reds, the greens,
It filled my eyes with wonder the best I have ever seen.
So though I only stopped to browse I'd checked up on my lolly
I found I was not completely broke, so I ran to get a trolley.
There were hollyhocks, forget-me-nots, all tempting me to buy.
Must take care, not overspend, I promised I would try.
Antirrhinums, Aquilegia, I will buy a box of each
I moved onto the roses, now I was looking for a peach
Delphiniums, Dianthus, I would buy a few of those,
I must move on, control myself or I would buy another rose,
Geranium Godetia, they all appear to me,
I must take care or once again I'd buy everything I did see.
I would make my way to checkout, it's been a frantic dash
I would unload my trolley and hope I'd got the cash!

R Giddings

JOURNEY

I felt the swell of a sapphire sea
Between the gentle Summer Isles.
It rolled and bellied into waves
And patterns of lace for many miles.

I saw the island's granite humps
Caressed with mist along their spines.
Jurassic shapes heaved into sky;
Older still than druid times.

I felt the brush of morning breeze
Whispering soft of island lore,
Of ancient folk and standing stones
Like chessmen on a hallowed floor.

I saw the flick of a seagull's wing
His screech, an awesome tale of past
Clannish wars and kilted men
Who battled to their bitter last.

I felt the peaty moors beneath
Where otters danced in rainbow lochs.
I watched the glow of midnight sun
And time stood still upon those rocks.

Gay Horton

NEVER ALONE!

I went shopping one wintry morning,
A face appeared,
Was it you my darling?
So, I put the shopping into my car,
Your smile appeared, you were not far,
I was driving alone one rainy day,
I heard a voice from far away,
So, I carried on that lonely road,
I thought of you, I was not alone.
It was a cold and icy afternoon,
I saw a vision, in the shape of the moon.
I walked on by to my surprise,
The shape of the sun came before my eyes.
One sunny day I was riding on my bike,
A cyclist appeared with much delight.
A message came to me via my phone,
It said, *remember, you're never alone.*
That night came and I put on the light,
The room lit up and it shone so bright.
That vision appeared and he sat beside me,
He said, 'Oh yes, my dear, it's me indeed.'

Yvette Avonda Rose

KENYA

As the ancient Baobab tree embraces the breeze
Where bullets from the British as they tried to seize
Land, left pockmarks on her bark as physical memories
I travel along the red ochre mud tracks from Tsavo West to East
Towards the rising sun on the trail to find a magnificent beast
They say it hasn't rained like this on October 10th in ten years
Ten days I am here to wash away my tears and conquer my fear
The more I travel these bumpy, man-broken roads; the more I feel she is near
The sun is hiding behind the clouds but closer, her heat is intense
The landscape of elephant-destroyed trees and bushes and rolling hills is immense
Evidence of a delicate ecosystem in such harmonious balance
Fields of crops were bare-feet women bend backs and slave till they drop; stop to wave
Little children with dark skin and ivory smiles reflecting the sun's rays
Brighten the day as they play, and shout jambo to us as we pass their way
Under the gaze of Mount Kilimanjaro
I fall in love with the vast life in Tsavo
I wanted adventure and experience and so it was meant to be
That we got stuck in thick, sinking mud up a torn steep hill in a vehicle that was smoking
dangerously
Local people came rushing, my panic was gushing, as they swiftly pulled my family to safety
I found myself suddenly in the middle of nowhere, aware of my vulnerability
As my fear was lifted by the Kenyan people's spirit and the gravity of their charity
I realised with new clarity the irony that our lives were saved by this poverty-struck community
As I jumped over a ditch, onto a bank to escape from a swerving out-of-control car
With help from a local woman with ripped clothes, muddy feet and the heart of a star
I felt humble as the encounter perceptively put my life into a different context
I had no idea the delay would lead to what happened next

It was twilight that day on the Savannah when the vision appeared
A lioness out of nothing ran and pounced at something and then disappeared
I rubbed my eyes and blinked, still hardly believing
What was this image my eyes were receiving? The strange light was deceiving
I must have imagined it, was the only conceivable reasoning
As the darkness fell I stood watching the water hole from the safety of the lodge I was in
When a mysterious growl sounded out in the night that made my heart start palpitating
I felt myself calling for my dream; this wish of meeting a lion out of captivity was captivating
I shone a torch but all I could see were light orbs exploding
Against the pure black darkness of the enchanting evening
The next day we crossed a railway on the way to the national park
Still haunted by the images that had left their mark
When I was told by my guide about the two massive mane-less male lions that years ago
Were known as The Darkness and The Ghost of Tsavo
They destroyed many who worked on the building of the iron snake; a bad omen fulfilled attack
Associated with a once ancient tribal prophecy by the Massai halted in its tracks

The mane-less only found in these parts is closer in shape and size to the prehistoric cats
My mind was still reeling from these astonishing facts
When I saw her on the rocks, free protected from Man, healthy and relaxed
As the lioness with her cubs refusing to hide, looked me in the eyes
I felt a tingle in my spine, she looked so divine, I nearly cried
She captured the essence of Kenya herself, so powerful, she filled me with pride
She had a scar through her left lunar eye, she was wild not savage
A Simba, a symbol, standing in the face of human ravage
We travelled along the Shimba Hills, the land of the leopard as the sun set
Feeling tired and weathered with the warm rain which endeavoured to get us wet
When she came to me as a woman I had already met
She carried the weight of her country on her head
And from the plains of the Serengeti, to the wonder of the Massai Mara
From the city of Nairobi to the famous coast of Mombasa
She led; her children from hardship with the drum beat of the Swahili
Along with the buffalo, bush babies and colobus monkey
Through the winds of corruption, drained resources, sweeping drought and the bite of malaria
Past petrol lorries, dangerous roads, foreign huntsman; whispering, 'Hakuna Matata'
To the umbrella trees and vegetation with healing properties
Inspiring the carvings from beautiful ebony
A beauty from disaster
They might be poor but with her on their side they have happiness and laughter
As the Indian Ocean, kisses her white sandy shores, populated by dolphins and ancient coral reef
I stare up at the North Star and I'm filled with belief
Like the knowing smile of the Massai chief
The moon appears yellow and so close to me now
To this poor African queen, I just have to bow.
I left a part of me in Kenya and took a piece of her home with me in its place with the tide
Asanti forever and in my heart the grace of the dark continent of Mother Africa will always reside.

Sarah Robertson

CONCEPTION

(For my parents, forgiveness is strength)

Not even a miracle can enhance a chance for bloodline heritage to convince me of another mother tongue.
A dark air of which I inhale, exhaled from birth, feeling my development was deceived from conception of which I formed strong beliefs of contraception
And continued my creation with minute family relations
And answers to questions I have not yet heard but answered myself
Still not even a miracle can enhance a chance for a bloodline heritage to convince me of another mother tongue.
I'm a real life experiment of life negligence finding truth
A product of unstableness and mixed cultures with did not group
I'm the evidence of a broken marriage, the third baby in a carriage
With no coverage but exposure to the knowing and growing of how *not* to raise children to fake fulfilment of food and toys
But bought affection of girls and boys fooled by conception but enabled my progression and knowledge to answer burning questions from birth
From the journey of the sperm and echoes felt where the womb failed to block out the sound and turns and in the genes it stated *this egg has been sedated*
Woman meets man, life expands but the issues are not resolved
The raw tissues of nature tears show bold as new baby girl is born, tears are cold
As she grows the entrance to life closes and the red roses to compliment the birth show unfragranced scent of a deceived conception
So the steps to expression formed in torn stages from the bad genes and sharp apparatus used to get me out of being a patient of a patient
A product of unstableness and mixed cultures which did not group
But brought me the truth of a mother tongue
Not even a bloodline heritage can convince me of any other.

Nadia Fahmy

AMID SUMMER SUN . . .

A mid bright summer sunlight suddenly a flash of whitest white against azure sky.
M y senses come alive so suddenly at this display of aerial
  delight . . .
I 'm entranced at once by the acrobatic display of dazzling deft flight.
D ropping in and out of sight, the silent, frenetic, frenzied silken wings of white.

S unlight shimmers onto this beauteous fleeting sight of a butterfly in flight . . .
U nder its spell I fall, entranced, amazed by a balletic dance of agility arrayed.
M any days have passed, before nature's priceless gift now I before me see,
M anifold reasons may I extol for this exquisite sight we now freely behold . . .
E ach fleeting wingbeat delights me more as into the sky a butterfly gently soars.
R iches beyond compare, are thus displayed for all to share amid a sunlit sky.

S uddenly as it came, now it passes out of sight to delight another's eyes . . .
U nder no illusions be, it's by God's grace such beauty and avidly embrace.
N othing more than sheer delight can one feel at this beauteous sight of a butterfly in excited
  flight on tissue-white wings.

Michael Counter

THE OLD HOUSE

They're pulling down the old house
And I often stand and stare
And think of all the life it's seen
When there were people living there
A little fire in every room,
To keep the children warm
The windows all shut tightly
Against the winter storm.
But now it hasn't got a roof
And the chimneys, they stand tall
It looks just like a skeleton
It hasn't even got a wall.
Soon there will be nothing left
To show that it's been there
And everybody will forget
Except the folk who once lived there.

Maureen Jones

MY PUPPET

You are the puppet,
I hold the strings.
I yank and I pull,
You will do the strangest of things.

As each arm creases,
Against the turbulent tide
Attract and repel,
Still obediently by my side.

You do not smile,
Though I tear away your frown.
I tug upwards but,
You continue to drown.

As each leg bends,
To dance at my command.
You reluctantly follow,
Under the shadow of my hand.

You are the puppet,
I hold the strings.
Interesting the sins,
That the heavy hearty brings,
As you, the sad puppet sings.

Emily Williamson

TAKE FIVE

When you've been
Driving your lorry
Across five continents,
Or flexing your muscles
With building work,
After a long day's
Graft you need to
Take stock and take a rest.
You need to place
Your head on that pillow
And just sit back and relax
With a cold beer
And a KitKat in your swollen hands
You need to go into a trance-like state
So close your eyes and enjoy the silence
After a hellish day
Looking after the kids
And preparing their dinner
You need to take it easy
Sit down
Instead of breaking your head in two . . .
Have a deep hot bath and take five.

Matthew Lee

GRAPEVINE

The grapes of wrath or grapes of wine?
Could e'er these two in harmony entwine?
Will one spread out hurtful news so false
As to alter someone's lifetime course?

Will one divulge news that is true
Or spread alarm and despondency?
Will one bring healing and a cure
Or undermine, and make unsure?

Our spoken thought and outward show
Taken up by hearers, eyes all aglow,
Mis-using such innermost knowledge
That could send one over the edge.

Such grapevines, ears clung to the wall,
Distorting words which may then appeal
Scarce can their message be believed
Reputations lost, ne'er retrieved?

So it would seem that there are those
Who earn our wrath when they disclose
Twisted facts of personal news
Changed by gossip to be untrue.

The grapes of wine be they white or red,
May indeed go to one's head
Though they may harm or they may hurt
They too grow up out of the dirt.

But malice is not part of those
Whose fruits are meant our souls to please
Token of a Saviour's gracious call,
His life and sacrifice for one and all.

Thus those grapes, inspired by his word,
Lead us to follow truth we have heard
And live creatively each and every day
By one who's The Vine and is The Way.

Jo Allen

THE CRY OF THE POOR

We are constantly put to the test,
And we have to do our best.
Every day we struggle,
In the desperate hope that it is nearly the end of our long fought battle.
We fight hard to survive,
To live, to breathe, just to stay alive!
We are all beaten and battered,
Our clothes worn and tattered.
Completely stripped of our pride,
We have absolutely nowhere left to hide.
Like rats we pathetically scratch and scramble for morsels of food,
Living lives, no human being should.
We are struggling just to attain the bare necessities,
With little or no available opportunities.
There is certainly no room for the weary or meek,
If survival is what you truly seek!
And that is the honest truth; for it is either fight or flight
You choose
However, in my opinion either way, you lose.
Oh but to what end?
Father your salvation please send,
From above, please bless with your love.
Take away all this suffering and sorrow,
And please give us hope for a better and brighter tomorrow.
But I do beseech you to make haste,
Before it is too late and we are all lying in utter and complete waste!

Lydia Gachuhi

MY SWEET

My sweet, I know you are asleep over there,
But I yearn to see you now.
To once again feel the softness of your hair,
To appreciate your olive skin,
In such ways only we knew how.

My sweet, who knows over there,
To nuzzle towards your neck, and inhale your bodily scent,
As though it's the first time they're breathing air,
As unwittingly and naturally as I have loved you,
For every embrace together we had spent.

My sweet. I will always think of you up there.
And I wonder about the moment that I might be with you.
Unless I am destined to drown below in my despair,
I'd thank God a thousand times a day,
If I could just return to you, my sweet.

Azize Bozkurt

FROZEN BEAUTY I

Skeletal trees hoar frost on their branches
Delicate tracery of dazzling white
Gleaming like crystal on a cold winter's morning
Displaying their beauty in new day's first light

Slowly built up through hours of darkness
Layer on layer all through the night
Greeting the morning with sparkling brightness
Such splendid finery, oh what a sight.

Sun climbing higher with dazzling brightness
Bringing forth warmth, drives the hoar frost away
Dripping wet branches have lost all their beauty
'Til night comes again and Jack Frost comes to play.

Ken Capps

THE GHOST OF YESTERDAYS

I walk these streets and what do I see?
I see my town: what was, what is, what always will be.
The new builds, renovations, the trappings of change,
The River Tyne, a constant, flowing through Northern veins.
Gone maybe the tenements, first school, the ballast hill,
But despite demolition, our identity holds still.
For here I stand before a corpse of our history;
The husk of the shipyard, defaced, skulking, pitifully,
Stripped inside and out, naked, laid bare,
But I look closely, something still lives there:
A fragment of paper clings on a wall,
Lines, numbers, words, a roll call.
Men, names, people, our ancestral kin;
Their souls and their spirits remain within.
Men of steel, sweat, blood and toil,
Are riveted into the metal, the brick and soil.
They may change this town, destroy it, renew,
Yet those long gone men live on, within me and you.
So tread the beaten pavements, but open wide your eyes.
As the ghosts of our yesterdays pass you by.
Keep them alive in our memories, hold tight to your past,
For the landscape may vanish, but heritage will last.

Claire Cruddas

SITTING HERE THINKING

Sitting here thinking of what we used to do,
I never could imagine that what you said was true,
I thought our love was special, but now I know it's gone,
Just sitting here thinking and wondering what went wrong.
If I could turn the clock back to when we were together,
I would make sure that it would last forever,
Just sitting here thinking about what we used to do
And hoping you'll remember the times I shared with you.

Tracy Ridley

THE WIND IS SINGING

The wind is singing to me
A song of sadness
A song of leafless woods
And a flowerless plain,
A song of biting frost
And of drifting snow,
A song of stinging hail
And of bitter rain.

The wind is singing to me
A song for heeding
'One day you'll go down in the dark
With no returning
Rejoice in the light
Find joy where joy is
Yield not to mourning,'

I will sing to the wind
A song of knowing
'Time holds wealth for me
In spite of seeming,
I have the moon and the stars
And the pearly dawn,
I have the misty dusk
And the night for dreaming.'

Eileen-Margaret Kidd

BUNTING

So this is the tavern. Hairy Rosie
at the bar pouring long shots for no one,

barmaids dripping, dangling over fans.
all of them stare at the man, empty man,

playing for pints under bunting hanging
blue denim and suede. Singing, with borrowed

pain and the empty pew beside me weeps
as he tells us all, clear, that to live here

is to take a very long time to die.

Natalie Rogers

I WILL MISS YOU SO MUCH MUM

(In memory of Nancy Shuttle)

On the 15th September, a part of me died,
From five in the morning all I could do was cry,
The hospital phoned and said my mum passed away,
Of all the sad things in my life this was my worst day,
I know everyone thinks they have the best mum
But I had the best, she was my mother, my chum,
She was there for me whether it was night or day,
No matter what I did, for her I can never repay,
For the love, the kindness and the happiness she gave me,
I'm so very proud to be a part of her family tree,
I'm missing you Mum, so very, very much,
I miss our nightly chats, and your gentle touch,
I miss your sense of humour, all the laughing we did,
All my adult life and even when I was a kid,
A part of me died the same time as you,
I feel empty inside and I don't know what to do,
At least you're not in pain now of that I'm so glad,
But I miss coming round to see you and I feel so sad,
Have a safe trip to Heaven and let the angels look after you,
They've got my job now and they'll know what to do,
But they will never love you the way I did and still do,
We had a special bond Mum and a love so strong and true,
You will live in my heart Mum, forever and a day,
We will meet again soon Mum, that day is not far away,
You go and see your mum and dad, and your hubby too,
They will keep you company till, I can be with you.

Leah Vernon

SYRIAN MELODY

Those pyramids of tears and flesh
Call me through the cold screens
My eyes are deaf
And ears are wrapped with the void
That screams silently
And is born with the smirks of the bullets
And I dance with the wounded wind
And rest in the teeth
Of those whom I knew once
As a child of history
And pain.

Amal Audeh

WRAP OFF, RAP ON

Take a stance,
Wave your arms, mumble quickly,
Wear baggy trousers, show your bum,
Impossible rhymes, swear profusely,
Get your fingers in silly positions,
Make a CD,
Make personal appearances,
Appear to have your head on back to front,
Stagger about,
Make sure nobody understands a single word,
Be outrageous, get mad applause,
Say your name is
Browning Keats Wordsworth dub
And don't forget to add a boring beat.

David Robinson

JUST ANOTHER DAY

Just another day, *bang, bang,* instantaneous death
Out of the blue, gone, departed, bereft, alone
The suddenness, the shock, reeling, stunned,
Cold, clammy fingers around my heart
My breasts heaving, heat pounding, lungs dredging,
Tears ebbing and flowing, dead, death, gone
Echoing in my mind, numbness, pinching myself,
Can this be true? Am I dreaming? No, this is certainty
Cold, I feel as cold as the grave, trembling,
Weak, I take a seat, now I feel sick, wobbly
Bang, bang, just an ordinary day.

Yet only a moment ago, normality, no sign
We were speaking of the day ahead and now!
My heart, my mind feeling only dread
Fear, complexity, bewilderment, so young!
Yes, comparatively, just 63 years, why you?
Why me? Floating, everything unreal on an
Unknown voyage, *bang, bang,* just another day
Now I hang suspended, unseeing, unbelieving
Holding onto the past, pushing the future away
Icy fingers down my spine shaking
Bang, bang, just an ordinary day.

Everything just a blur, staring at nothing
I must pull myself together, I have to cope
I feel my body heavy, unable to move
How shall I cope? Where do I start?
Someone is asking my name, what is my name?
Where do I live? How can I live alone?
I look at them askance, just an ordinary day!
I want to hide away, why, why now, why us?
Why me? *Bang, bang*, instantaneous death
I'm so pleased he didn't suffer. I am helped to my feet
Just another day, in an ordinary life, in any street.

Susie Sullivan

THE DRUMS

The High Surdo
I am High Surdo, slim and long.
Percussion is my song.
Played within the band.
Friends on ev'ry hand.
Oh, hear the drums so loud.
Draw in the festive crowd!

The Snare, a brother drum,
Which sounds so all should come.
To hear the drums so loud.
Draw in the festive crowd.

The large drums and the small,
The beat of drums for all.
Oh, hear the drums so loud,
Draw in the festive crowd!

The Snare
I'm Snare drum, my beat's great,
And I and my drum mates,
Love to sound out loud,
Within the joyful crowd

The Timbre
The Timbre sounds as well,
So soon we all can tell,
That makes the drums so loud,
Draw in the happy crowd!

The Tamberet
The merry Tamberet,
Does not like getting wet.
But plays with all, proud,
Before the merry crowd!

The Samba
The Samba, tunes so well,
That soon we all can tell
And see the cheerful crowd,
Dance to the drums so loud!

The Drums
The drums, we play so strong,
Percussion is our song.
So thus, we drums so loud,
Delight the festive crowd!

Peter Morey

MUM DON'T GO!

Mum I'm here staring at you, begging you not to go
I beg you, please stay; I need you here with me
I'm sorry for all the pain I caused you, all the hurt you felt

Why now Mum, why you got to go?

Please just give me one more day to make my wrongs right
I beg you please, don't leave
Mum I'm here on my knees; tears are falling down my cheeks

Mum pray with me, I said pray with me

God I kneel before you; please just hear me; please listen to what I say
I'm here to repent all my sins
I know I did my mum wrong
I caused the hurt, the pain, the stress, the worries
Now she lies here and I don't know what to do
So I came to you at my darkest time
So just hear me out, give me the time
Even if it's only one night

Mum, just stay awake 'cause I need you
Mum, just give me the blame
I'm sorry for the weed you smelt
All the nights I stayed away and didn't even bell
I know that must have caused you stress

Sorry for all the hits you felt, I never should have hurt you with my belt
I'm sorry for the time you did
All because of the gun I hid in your drawer, next to your sleeping pills and all the bills

Mum, please don't go, I need your forgiveness so I can remove the guilt.

Russeni Fisher

THANK YOU GIRLS

I have six lovely granddaughters
Amy, Katie, Lucy, Chloe, Sophie and Hannah
They all mean the world to me
And are very helpful to their Nana

Whenever we are together
They brighten up my day
And really make me chuckle
At the priceless things they say

They once asked if I was a little girl
When the dinosaurs were here
My answer to that question was
'I just missed them by a couple of years.'

Over the years they have given me drawings
Cards and letters too
Little poems and stories
So thanks to all of you.

All these things I will keep forever
I love you all so much
You really are six smashers
I think you're *fabulous*.

Jackie Richardson

PARADISE LOST

They're fast losing the skills of hunting
Which must be said is hardly surprising –
In the forest where they live, there's a dearth of animals:
Apes and monkeys, honey badgers, porcupines;
These used to be their staple diet
Now you rarely see them roasting meat.

The Baka are a minority tribe,
It's the Bantu people running the show.
The loggers move in, the tees are felled,
There's money in mahogany.
As for this pygmy clan who have always dwelt
In this verdant paradise, they don't count.
Now cobalt will be mined from under the ground

Their future points even more to extinction,
Not hunting, how do they spend their time?
Drinking strong liquor that poisons mother's milk
And arouses fierce passions within their breasts.
See them fight like tigers amongst themselves.

They set off to find the 'Elephant mirrors'
Those pools where the pachyderms examine their tusks.
Encircled by hosts of lustrous butterflies
A father says to his daughter, 'Remember this,'
A way of life is confided to memory
Because that is all these people will have.

Tony Sainsbury

SOMETIMES NEVER MIND

Wishing nothing but to dissolve
And melt away, and soar upon
The wind across the cliffs and open shore
And out, over the sea,
Endless, stretching deepest blue
to somewhere else,
To somewhere else, brand new.

For never mind me.
Never mind the sky and setting sun,
The memories will last, despite the hurt
And I promise that all will be fine
And I promise that all the mistakes will no longer matter.
For really, *never mind me.*
Never mind me at all.

'Forget me not,' the flowers said,
Their blue faces upturned as you watched
The final birds crest the crashing waves
And out, out and away, they chase,
Towards the horizon. *All that way out there.*
I told you they would follow me,
Whispered it once, merely
Quiet, insignificant words
And now I hope you understand them.

Old friend. How unlike you to be so still,
Do not weep, and do not wonder.
For I am there, you know I am,
Somewhere like this, but so very
Far away. You won't forget, I know,
Because lasting in the end is all we can do.
Lasting and lasting and simply breathing
As the time flies and flies and carries on,
The ticking clocks and passing years
'Til all has changed and everything has wandered
On to somewhere else. *Like I did.*

I faded and I became the mist, the fog,
The grey haze,
I dwelt in places never seen or felt before.
Sometimes it lasts, sometimes it simply won't.
Never mind eh. *Never mind.*

Wishing nothing but to dissolve
And melt away, and soar upon
The wind across the cliffs and open shore
And out, over the sea,
Endless, stretching deepest blue
to somewhere else
To somewhere else, brand new.

Glynnis Morgan

HARD WORDS

The remit read, 'No singing, no dancing
- Just the power of the pen'.
A rather odd sort of challenge
- Since I don't know when!

Yet the 'Power of the pen
- is mightier than the sword'.
Whatever the subjects,
I oft take on board.

For I'll bring to your notice,
All that which is news,
In verses that rhyme,
I will proffer my views.

You may not always like,
The facts I relate,
About politicians and bankers,
Even heads of state!

I won't pull my punches,
Unlike those in 'the press',
Who kowtow to their editors,
'The truth', then suppressed.

Peter Mahoney

COMMUNICATION

What goes on inside
is Rachmaninov.
Romance, tenderness,
lyrical swell
and emotion,
so much emotion.

What goes on between us
is an advertising jingle,
practical
succinct
mundane even.

How do I bring what is inside,
outside;
show you my heart,
my inner life.

Would you want to see it
anyway?

Or is the mundane,
the contained
the practical,
enough for you.

Or is it just that
it is safe,
all you can deal with
in the hectic crush
of every day.

There have been moments
when the inner and outer touched.
When around us was enough peace
for me to reveal
and you to see
and not feel burdened.

Oh God, help us to create
and cherish those moments,
and feed on them
in the hectic crush
of every day.

Theresa Mundy

A SHORT ESSAY ON CHILDREN'S PLAY

I chanced to glance from a window
at children playing in the street below;
their colourful antics took me back
to halcyon times of myth and magic;
I couldn't resist opening the window,
setting sail on waves of wicked laughter
to a bay where cliffs of ivy trellis
rose above a stormy sea of long grass.

The garden shed, a mighty galleon,
we handkerchief pirates bearing down,
makeshift swords ready and able,
all hands to the oars of a cast-off table;
we'd meant to take no prisoners,
but time and tide got the better of us;
heaven closed in, fired a broadside
and our mothers called us back inside.

From the window I saw someone
rush at the children, moving them on;
'Away! Let's have some peace!'
(Leviathan jaws homing in on innocence.)
I slammed the window shut, angry
at being dragged thus from my reverie
if mindful that imagination's pull
has no place around a boardroom table.

I had a fight on my hands that day,
to see my motion passed come what may,
sailed too close to the wind in the eyes
of those least inclined to be adventurous,
but, oh, I got the better of them all
(in spite of a broadside too close to call)
steered my prize safely to harbour,
wiping my brow with a pirate's bandana.

R N Taber

EXAMINATION

A humid grey morning
In June
In the hall
Of stifled coughs
And rustling papers
Students are writing
Rows of heads
Bowed in concentration

The sound of raindrops
Splattering the window
Echoes the ticking
Of the clock
High up
On the wall

Stony-faced invigilators
Pace silently
Up and down
The rows
Of scribbling students

The clock ticks
Rain splatters
Through hours
Of stifled coughs
And rustling papers

Then

Pens down!

Necks unbend, heads rise
Sighs escape
Outside the rain stops
Clouds part
And sunshine
Lightens the day.

Rachel Sutcliffe

THE BLACK STALLION

Strong and defined with lines of clean shave
The roughness of his manners immensely captivating
The lazy huskiness of the voice so intoxicating to the mind
His reasoning makes the foolish words of the world wise
His looks create a new definition to being ugly
On the top of the hill he stands with such valour
With his armour ready to strike with all charms alert
Details so profound that cannot be mistaken
Tall and masculine for the mare to observe
The black stallion defined as beautiful
Walks with such aura and dignity within each step taken
He laughs with a spoken and shameless strength
And talks with authority in each sentence said
A moment spent with him gives the impression of a déjà vu
His street name can be called stubborn as can be seen from his different strokes
The black stallion has no time to waste once his mind is made up

For once a mare touches the nerve of desire all resolution is made
The black stallion makes no disguise of his feelings for the other
Expresses his desire in intensity perceived as a show off.
He comes like a thief in the night to steal the heart, which he desires
Unlike the thief, he cares deeply
The black stallion, a figure of strength, audacious charisma and mystery
By principles conquering principalities,
The strides of the black stallion – guided by the One Almighty

Even though the stallion stands strong and masculine
It cannot be ignored the arrogance of the stallion in manners of approach
Like an animal from the desert he approaches the mare
No manner of subtleness can be accounted for wooing the mare
Selfish and none compromising in any relationship formed
Willing to take but never to sacrifice as termed as the stallion
Rugged in manner of love and terms love making as a complete definition of romance
Forgets romance can be classified as a lot of things which includes the needs of a mare
More calm as ever decides if the stallion would be her destiny or not
She resolves within the need to shape the stallion to meet her needs would be a concern.

Ibiere Addey

DUVETS

The missus said, 'Let's get a duvet,'
As I quietly sipped at me drink,
'And a cover with frills round the edges,
And flowers on a background of pink.
A fifteen tog min's what we'll go for,
Cos we don't see that much of the sun,
It'll save us a mint on electric,
Cos a duvet costs nothing to run.'

The very next Saturday lunchtime,
She dragged me off out round the shops,
I could have been sat at home watching
The snooker being shown on the box!
Quite soon, we were lost in the world of
The big hollow-fibre filled quilt,
And me head was soon going in circles,
And me wallet was starting to wilt!

There were bleedin' great goose-down filled thick 'uns,
And others not quite so dense,
And the missus was talking of tog mins,
Like the whole flippin' business made sense!
And then it was valences, covers,
And pillows and curtains as well.
In fact, every sort of accessory
That the salesman wanted to sell.

They loaded me up like a pack-horse,
'Til I couldn't see which way to go,
And I staggered and wobbled back homewards
Under three tons of shopping or so.
Then when we got home, bloody knackered,
The misses said, 'Let's try it out,
It won't take us more than half-hour,
And probably less, I've no doubt.'

It was just three o'clock when she said it,
We started the job with a will:
By quarter-past-seven that evening,
We were bloody-well hard at it still!
A gigantic king-size marshmallow
Takes someone with four arms to hold,
While two other four-armed assistants
Try getting the cover unrolled.
As fatigue gets a grip on the biceps,
The problems are ten-fold increased,

And the exercise takes on the aspect
If dancing with someone deceased!
When the whole job was finally finished,
We both flopped right out of the bed,
All puffing and panting and wheezing,
And feeling done-in and half-dead.

Then the missus said, 'P'haps we should test it,'
With a twinkling look in here eye,
Then started removing her clothing,
And quick as a flash, so did I:
I never realised that a duvet
Could give so much pleasure and fun.
Cos there was me thinking a duvet
Was a basin for washing your bum.

Mick Nash

SWEET, SWEET SUMMER

In summer I get up early,
The air is soft and tender
Brief respite from life's hurly-burly
To peace my thoughts surrender.
Goodbye to cough and wheezes,
And strange, embarrassed poses.
To quell my frequent sneezes,
And stop these running noses.
Trips to the seaside looming,
Shop prices steeply soaring.
Loud fairground noises booming,
The thunder clouds keep roaring.
The temperature is rising,
Grass dries to stark bare patches.
A heatwave, that's surprising,
Brings sunburn that almost matches
And skin that keeps on shredding.
It's getting even hotter,
My body heat, now spreading,
Soaks in the heat like butter.
In summer I go to bed very late,
And pray that night is chilling,
May sleep the heat abate,
Sweet dreams the heat distilling.

Jack Scrafton

A DAY THAT DOESN'T BRING YOU

Is like a millpond of mediocrity
A daze recurring
It's like peeling wallpaper offending
My sunlight eye
It's like cobwebs massing militia style
In the corners of my imagination
It's a drought in my saline drip-feed of wellbeing.
It's like a daffodil imitating a mole
No direction home
It's a blister on beauty
A shackle on beast
A tough decision never made
A contemplation rudely interrupted
It's like a light switched on in my head that cries help
It's like a muddied swimming pool in my guts
With laughing sharks and razor teeth
It's like the almighty learning violin next door
It's like a poem I may never write but will never forget
It's like a honking sock pulled down over my head
Like a carnival mask with a dread of terrorism
It's firework night in a hospital
A hearse with an empty coffin
Stuck in traffic
It's a vampire bloodsucking the innocents
It's suffocation from the half lifetime
And judgeful eyes that would separate us
It's another line from 'It's like this Doc'
When I see you common sense would try to ride a paper plane
Over the Grand Canyon
It's now in French
S'il vous plait, mois excuse
You are even after all
My treasured muse.

Carl Strohmeier

MAGIC BLACK BOX

My magic black box in corner sits adorned with me to you bears
Mostly vacant screen, dark as night, concealing secrets it shares
Revolutionary digital TV, widescreen, HD ready
Unlike its predecessor, dumpy rotund tubby tele
Its sleek linear lacquered design seems somewhat out of place
Midst the floral, butterflies, lavender, pink, Paddington Bear and lace
Brain train transport to boundaries beyond, refuelling imagination
Thoughts, ideas, insights into alternative written creation

Merest touch of detached button gadget, vivid imagery commences
Sound and sight, colour bright, bombardment of heightened senses
Latest confrontation crisis down in Albert Square
Medical feats, sitcom repeats, security breach for spooks to repair
Costume period dramas flirt with courtship, love, romance
Detective trails, X Factor trials, live tennis tension enhanced
TARDIS journey of escapism from papered walls confined
QVC shopping, Mentalist channel hopping to stimulate enclosed mind

Third party life provider controlled by schedule of programme
Window to nation, news information, temporary reprieve from how I am
Enhanced existence, cloned assistance, fictional lives on loan
Borrowed adventures, educational venture, information now known
Click of Dorothy's red painted shoes, someplace to go that's not home
Remote control living from bedroom division, a world wide inside to roam
Pause live TV for a cup of tea, a conjured film to recall
My illusionist black box in corner sits, magic entertainment and all.

Shirley Clayden

MY WEE BROTHER GEORGE

I wanted to write down something
Truly from the heart
So I got my pen and paper
And tried to make a start
But I was truly troubled
And this stirred around my head
Cos I could not believe
That Georgie Podgie was dead,
They murdered him on a park bench
By setting him in flames
They printed it in the papers
And called him horrid names
They were calling him a tramp
Which really wasn't true
Too proud to go a begging
It really wouldn't do,
So I would like them to explain
The meaning of the word
As I think it's truly insulting
And really quite absurd
To die in such a dreadful way
It really is a shame
I don't know where the fault lies
But I need someone to blame.
These people are truly evil
And have no thought for life
They killed my brother for no reason
And it cuts me like a knife
Whatever is seen to be done
It will not bring George back
And all because of barbarity
And a single wicked act,
Material things meant nothing
As he was grateful for what he'd got
But George had more than me and you
And it was something that can't be bought
He never brought us trouble
He never gave us grief
So he has earned his peace in Heaven
And that's my strong belief
He looked so peaceful as he lay
Although it was distressing
God had taken his pain away
And had given him his blessing

My brother was human, decent and kind,
He didn't have trouble or malice in mind.
I can't imagine what happened that night,
When two mindless lads set him alight,
They thought it was funny to torch his head,
It was done for a laugh, one of them said,
How can this happen in this modern day?
Is this how children learn how to play?
But they went on trial, to learn their fate
'Cause they had won, for George it was too late,
But even in court they had no shame.
They gave each other all of the blame,
Those boys perceived my brother as a tramp,
So he was given that horrible stamp,
I had apologies from the newspapers each and every one,
But for me it was too late, the damage had been done.
They not only killed him, they tarnished his name,
He was known as a tramp, his claim to fame,
But no one has the right to label this way
What right do they have to say what they say?
I saw things I wished I never saw
In that so-called court of law,
George's things were in a plastic packet,
Burnt, stuck together, his jumper and jacket,
I thought I'd throw up, at this stage
With all of that evidence, page after page,
They committed a truly barbaric crime,
So they should be punished, and do the time
But you mark my words and wait and see,
They get a smack on the wrists and a colour TV,
We're paying our taxes, for the likes to be taught,
But what are we teaching? I've lost the plot,
George must have suffered so much that night,
I can't bear to think, it fills me with fright,
Those boys have been pampered, a pat on the head,
They don't give a damn that my brother is dead.
But they have been found guilty and rightly so,
Yet they won't be better adults, when they're free to go,
They'll be out and about, having served a short time,
Well it was only murder, it's hardly a crime
The trial is over, justice has been done
We can all go home now, well all except one:-
My wee brother George!

Susan Johnstone

TRUE LOVE

You took my hand and led me to,
A place where dreams you can't undo,
Our hearts entwined, too deep to break,
True hope for promises we'd make.

I found you when my life was low,
And now can't bear to let you go,
My thoughts, my dreams, my hopes are you,
And love like this is all too few.

Although our paths lay worlds apart,
These risks we've taken from the start,
Our feelings deep, so true, so strong,
How can a love like this be wrong?

The thought of days without you here,
Without your touch, your body near,
I feel a pain, a loss inside,
As though some part of me has died.

I knew that from that moment on,
I would be lost if you were gone,
And all our memories from the start,
I'd give to you so you won't part.

A perfect memory on every line,
Of amazing days when you were mine,
And you'll read it back and then you'll see,
True love is us, just you and me.

Debbie Langham

FRIENDSHIP

A good friend is very hard to find,
One who touches your heart.
Someone who is understanding and kind,
With whom you never want to part.
A good friend lifts you up high
When our world is blue.
Is there when others pass you by,
Takes care and comforts you.
A good friend is one who knows your faults,
But loves you just the same.
Listens to your highs and lows.
But always plays the game!
Yes a true friend is always there
To share life's rugged way.
A shining gem beyond compare,
To treasure every day.

Josie Rawson

THE SWING

The swings were empty. I lifted you
And sat you safe in the enclosed seat
And I pulled you back as far as I could pull.
And then I let you go.

Was that the first time I let you go?
You went forward and then you came back to me
And I pushed you away from me.
Was that the first time I pushed you away?

I pushed you forward again and again
And always you came back to me;
Higher and higher and harder and harder
And still you always came back to me.

I pushed you into stomach-wrenching flight,
Harder and harder and higher and higher,
And you saw things that I, rooted, could never see.
And then? What then? Will you still come back to me?

Leslie Scrase

THE PORTAL

March wet winds, azure angels morning blue, swept down,
Deft darters dashing through tall long-needled pines,
Lighter green than evergreen, as everything did leap and dance.
Tiny gold-dust, star-glint-glitter sun flashed, flowed down
To dazzle my eyes, provoke sweet wrenching pain inside
My heart-leap to wax me warm while waltzing wind
Swirled in spring and merrily nudged the spring in
Every step-stride I stretched along the squishy
Green and tickle-buzzed my ear with eager expectation
New transforming, thrilling marvels now awaited me.
Heavy university texts I lugged became supremely light.
Grimaced gargoyle halls' phantasmal monsters,
Whinnying with the winds' will dispelled their mystery
When within the tumult suddenly the sun burst, blazed
And blinded me and when thereafter sight returned,
She faced me laughing then, shouting through her tears.
I didn't have to find you – she cried – *Here you are!*
You told me goodbye years ago – I sighed – *You've come far?*
You needed me – she nodded – *You called me in the wind.*
Can we go somewhere to be alone? A place we can attend
To all this day has led us to, like some pilot star?
Warm as Baltic amber, her auburn hair glowed in the light
While soft and plush as deepest sable her dark eyes smiled
Wrapping me in easy joy before her arm wrapped round my waist.
My car is down the hill – I said – *We can go there.*
Ah! – she laughed and tugged my hand – *We can go anywhere.*
Being one part in some vast whole surely atoms are even aware,
But only man and woman joined can fill the entire universe.
Concord soft and warm is wind and light, rain and clear,
Power at its vortex, calm and storm, safety, peace and fear.
I took her to my home even though we were already there,
Seated her on my sofa, turned on the song and sat beside her.
I bless the day I found you – the singer began. She smiled up
At me and gazed into my very soul while I went on like the wind.
She let me talk, prattle on, till I reached that one last sentence
When I bemoaned how sad it was our timing was so wrong for us.
Still, I hung my head in joy that she was near and all she was
Seemed to embrace me, surround me as breathing perfumed mist.
You matter more than matter and light is only metaphor for God –
She said – *Yet there are things you must know, paths to be trod,*
Doors you must pass truly through, however untimely and odd,
Or you will die, truly die, your matter never matter, only a façade
To fall in dust, never beyond the metaphor the light be seen to nod.
Suddenly her lips pressed mine, a fire-burn branding me for all time.

Kisses I had known before but I'd never known one kiss like these
As we became that universe, body, soul and all we'd ever be.
When I awoke she had gone; yet, her dew was still upon me
And I reclined so joyfully in the chilly air all in new nakedness.
Beside me lay a perfumed note, I raised it up and it read:
A gift of grace – to leave us free, but I will not return you'll see.
My friend has come and taken me, but hold my love, I give it free,
And know as you go on alone, my love remains a certainty
And know if I go on alone, you will ever be a part of me.
I wept in sadness for time's decay would even take the dew away.
Sunlight spilled through the open door to cascade at my feet
While March wet winds, azure angels morning blue, swept down.

March wet winds, azure angels evening blue, swept down.
Deft darters dashing through tall long-needled pines,
Darker green than forest green, as everything did leap and dance.
Tiny silver star-glint-glitter moon-flashed, flowed down
To overawe my eyes, provoke sad wringing pain inside
My heartstrings to freeze my flesh whilst biting wind
Swirled in spring and shrilly struck the spring in
Every step-stride I stretched along the squishy churchyard
Green and grated, rasped, my ear with edgy expectation
Deep transforming, ill-starred wonders now awaited me.
Light line-ruled logs I carried became unbearably heavy.
Greying curious church walls' glancing spectral shadows
Waving with the dying sun's rays, rushed round hazy hills
When, within their twirl, suddenly a sun-spark, shimmered,
Struck a gravestone on the slope beyond the church there
And beckoned like a firefly flitting to her muted air.
I didn't have to find you – I deeply sighed – *Here you are!*
I'm the sexton. We spoke, yes? – a man replied – *You've come far?*
You're the one I need – I nodded – *I called this afternoon.*
Can we go there now before the dark? May we see it soon
Before the evening light deserts the moon and star?
Jet as blackest lignite, his dark hair swallowed up the light
While hard and bright as shiny anthracite his dark eyes shone
Surrounding me uneasily in eerie twilight before he spoke.
The grave is up the hill – he said – *We can hurry there.*
Ah! – I exclaimed and followed him – *I knew it would be there.*
Bestriding the Earth as a footstool is the separate man's desire,
But man and woman asunder know fragmentation's dark despair,
Discord, hard and cold as stone and night, sharp pains and blocks,
Chaos at the vortex, stress and squall, the dangers, shards and rocks.
I struggled up the hilltop behind the sexton there, and
Stopped by the light as he turned his torch upon the grave beside us.
I bless the day I found you – the epitaph began. I frowned out

At him and stared into his solemn face while he read on like the wind.
I let him talk, prattle on, till he reached that one last sentence
Where he bemoaned how sad it was death came so soon for her.
Then, I hung my head in sorrow, she was here (and had come here
Soon after she'd embraced me) surrounded now by rising mists.
You matter more than matter and light is only metaphor for God –
She'd said – *Yet there are things you must know, paths to be trod,*
Doors you must pass truly through, however untimely and odd,
Or you will die, truly die, your matter never matter, only a façade
To fall in dust, never beyond the metaphor the light be seen to nod.
Deeply her lips had pressed mine, a fire-burn branding me for all time.
If I'd not known her kiss, my will would not have stood my lonely life
Though extortion and power tried to cleave the universe we had been.
My thoughts awoke, she had not gone and I felt her dew now upon me
And I stood still so blissfully in the chilly air in all new nakedness.
Beside her lay an empty space, I turned my head and said,
That vacant space – is it free? Will you check it out and then tell me?
It's taken – he said *She purchased it, for a friend she loved devotedly.*
The name? – I pled – *Who is the one, the one she loved so certainly?*
He spoke the name, I bowed my head and softly said – *I am he!*
I wept with joy for time's decay would never take the dew away.
Moonlight spilled down the sloping hill cascading below my feet
While March wet winds, azure angels evening blue, swept down.

Edgar Wyatt Stephens

FOOTPRINTS

The fog fermented outside as I came into class, not quite sterile enough for the tales that they told, to regale our young minds, through the dank dread of waiting for break. It was about a god and his son, ashore on the sand. Hand in hand, teacher said. A cacophony of giggles from the girls and all poignancy was lost. The footprints beside the son had dissipated, along with hope at times when the vagaries of life, of contentment and loneliness, tormented him, and brotherhood orbited, visible and constant, yet isolated from reach. But all was well for the father had carried him. Amen. The story was met with a chorus of maudlin rapture from the mouths, before they went back to chewing gum, not knowing that epiphanies are dumb when they're just given to you.

But the fog cleared, and summer was punctuated by a spattering of days upon Quantock hills, where I arrived as a static observer of beauty, and left with it stashed away in my pulse. In a launch across the mud, I lost a trainer in the caress and pull of the ground, and I did not care, for there I saw that it was saving me, from behaving, donning blue lumps that I've never been convinced that I need. My sole beats down, a stencil from my hobbit feet left indelibly on the ground and myself, a dialogue found. And I still haven't decided, nature, whether I am mine or yours. But you are the undisputed carrier.

Megan Sherman

THE TREASURE CHEST

Laughter swings from side to side,
As they charge their way up the stairs.
The thundering footsteps and breathless banter,
Immediately engulf the calm for another hour.
The pirates burst through the gates of the unknown,
And the search for treasure begins once again.

I see through their eyes like windows,
Inquisitive minds are working.
Rhythmically regular, robust and developing,
Like industrial machines with promises of silver.
They march to their places, one by one,
With mountainous bags over minuscule bodies.

I take them through this journey,
Unlock the treasure chest.
From solar flares to polar bears and so much more within,
It dances around the room, waiting to be claimed.
I watch them take what's theirs with pleasure,
As they grab every idea, every word and every fragment.

For now my work is done,
And yet they've only just begun.
So long is the voyage before them,
So many adventures to share.
And once again the wave of calm approaches,
As they disappear down the stairs.

Usha Hirani

AGEING

How the years have slipped
Like sharp splintered glass,
Moving so rapidly away
From the discarded past.
Yet, here in my own mind,
I am still young and free.
There are neither scars nor tears,
And this heartache cannot be.
I skip along an alternative path.
I plan by day and plot by night,
Watching the sun rise to greet
When all dream birds take flight.

Diana Kwiatkowski Rubin

DIAMOND JUBILEE

A toast to Her Majesty the Queen
From 1952 and all years in-between
From the splendour of her coronation
To her Diamond Jubilee celebration
With her nation's boundless admiration
For her indomitable spirit and dedication
A steadfast and constant dutiful reign
With grace and beauty, Elizabeth by name.
Your Majesty, Queen Elizabeth II
We, your subjects, respect and salute you
This momentous occasion overflows with jubilation
Confirming the country's unwavering devotion
Ma'am on this your diamond jubilee year
With rousing cheers, from far and near
We will always hold you dear
Britannia's icon, we love and revere

Ian Tomlinson

RISE AND FALL

Nobody knows, nobody goes,
Anywhere away, what people say,
Are you aware? 'Cause she don't care,
Who shows face, who wins the race.

Can you smile, walk a mile,
Run around the block? It's a shock,
The system blows, a runny nose,
Who wants you there? We don't care.

Prime Minister, a political blister,
On the nation's heel, won't do a deal,
So we shout, when you're about,
The bells won't ring, and we don't sing.

We want a revolution, for the generation,
Happy days were yesterday, that's what I say,
As the sun went down, to the smiling clown,
Jester cries for a thousand years, for all the broken years.

The cardboard cities, other side of the riches,
Cross the street to avoid, so we get annoyed,
Government who are you? Promises we never knew,
If you abandon us, who then can we trust?

You're all the same, to you it is just a game,
You could not care less but we will not rest,
United your downfall will be, just wait and see,
The dream of our freedom, will one day come.

Barry Clarke

UNTITLED

When candle burns with softly warm flame
Dark shadows fade to gentle shade of perfect light
Your presence near spreads warmth throughout a lonely heart
And completes it in a way that makes my soul delight.

(Alas if flame were ever to fade
I think my heart would break
To live without your candle's light
I would be a lonely fate)

When angel's wings unfold to shield a troubled heart
All problems fade like distant memories of the past
Your loving arms bring comfort to a mind distressed
And quell my tears from empty cries to joyful laughs.

(Alas if wings were to close
That fate I could not bear
Without the comfort of your arms
My heart would surely tear)

When sunlight breaks the heaviest, deepest, darkest cloud
All shadows flee the brilliance of its light
It's in this overwhelming love I find my joy
And I know for sure it's you with whom I'll share my love.

(Keep your candles ever burning
And I shall ever burn mine own
And in this warmth we'll soundly sleep
Knowing we will never need to feel alone).

Renie Sinclair

THE COMPLICATED WORKINGS OF THE MIND

The complicated workings of the mind escape to seek what you must find and all the time you're sitting here just struggling to arrive at what you always feared.

The meaning of your life is clear that space between every year means that you and I are no longer near.

So together we are strong and force the broad and long but apart the world just disappears as if you and I were never really here.

So walk away, and every step you become less and less part of what I've loved once and the differences between us and them are forever gone as all the time we have lived so long but have forgotten what the mind started to escape from.

The young man that met someone and fell in love then left behind his darkest song to be again a mind that's strong, now with the broadest of strokes and feelings of which are free to go and come.

Peter Kiggin

A DREAM DIVINE

'Twas dream divine,
In this soul of mine,
All of sacred song,
Doth the theme prolong,
As in ancient days,
Singing wondrous lays,
When the church bells rang,
And the angels sang.
'Twas at Christmas tide,
They their Lord denied.
As in stable bare,
He was born to share,
A world of loss,
Die upon a cross,
Come then souls of men,
Write with mortal pen,
Of the Christ who died,
Jesus crucified,
'Twas the son of God,
Like as roses rod,
And a man of faith,
Died a martyrs death,
Glory, hallelujah.

Peter Buss

MURMURATION RAPTURE

It's as if the spirit whispered 'Woman, why do you weep?
Gaze upwards to the heavens,
And feel rapture from the birds of the air.'

It was like a storm approaching,
The sky turned black above a skyline of trees,
This cloud grew darker, denser.

It then vanished behind a sloping hill,
Rapidly appearing again, with a mind, body and a life of its own,
First turning this way and that, as it moved quickly through the air.

Spreading throughout the sky like thick black lace,
Each separate entity using telepathic thought,
Shape shifting itself, into doves, ribbons and snakes.

Each mighty, segment all knowing
How the other particles in this cloud will move next,
As it came closer, ever closer.

The rhapsody caused a loud choir of chattering voices,
Then came a great sighing and whooshing,
A symphony, of many thousand wings.

An aerobatic display performed by a murmuration of starlings,
Across a twilight sky,
Suddenly the dark entity dropped to roost overnight.

A parliament of owls begin their haunt,
As a star glistens in a naked sky.

Josephine Smith

SINGING FOR BILLY GRAHAM

How bleak this grassy cold River Stour,
And Sudbury's hail in freezing April –
Thick winter coat, train to Liverpool Street,
City Line from Bank to Waterloo,
And catch the Hounslow train for ½ hour.
One stop past Putney, mauve and white lilac trees in bloom,
The gardens are full of pink and white apple blossom,
Everywhere is full of spring and flowers;
We were getting depressed with constant winter;
Then Hounslow, and I make my way to Holy Trinity Church,
The restaurant closes at 5pm,
So off to have a quick hamburger,
'You're going to Holy Trinity, they went to Taize at Christmas'
I make my way to Holy Trinity Church
'Can't sit where you sat for Louis Paleau rehearsals,
They are all altos sitting there,
Sit over there with the sopranos.'
'Start with psalm34, Oh taste and see how gracious the Lord is
The lions do lack and suffer hunger,
But they that seek the Lord shall lack nothing
The Lord redeemeth the soul of his servants,
And none of them that trust in Him will be desolate.'
'We'll sing Bless His Holy Name,
Went down well at the last Billy Graham rally
Then I love you Lord – no you must all get it right,'
I love you Lord, goes on till 9pm
And I have to leave –
Woman beside me had a streaming cold,
No don't worry, you won't catch the cold,
She came from Greenford Church Group, it's hay fever.
Woman on the other side is helping her husband
Sitting with the tenors in the row in front.
I tore up to Hounslow East bus garage
No 37 bus to Richmond and 9.45 train.
My train terminates at Sheffield
An Eastern Counties bus laid on
I see Barclays Bank Kelveden from window,
Two doors away, 'Charles Hadden Spurgeons lived here.'
Oh I've seen Springer's house at last.

Gladys Burgess

I'VE NO REPLY

White contrails cross the summer sky
At heights so great the human eye
Cannot make out the actual 'plane,
   unless the sun on metal glints,
      showing machine and people fly
         off where?! . . .
To which I've no reply.

At times, it's been me passing by,
Perhaps, far down below, to spy
Not single people, but a town
   and wonder what its name might be,
      who lives there and the reasons why
         they do . . .
To which I've no reply.

The silver speck's no longer nigh,
Its contrail broadens, soon to die
As moisture droplets in a wind
   I cannot hope to ever feel,
      because it blows so very high,
         a gulf . . .
To which I've no reply.

Still closer, though, two 'worlds' might lie,
Closeness does not contact imply,
For many things, effectively
   as forty thousand feet of air
      can any real meeting deny,
         a grief . . .
To which I've no reply.

When last breaths from the body sigh,
As heart and lungs no longer try
To keep this mortal frame alive,
   how wide's the step that I shall take? –
      'within the veil' I cannot pry,
         just trust . . .
In God and *His* reply.

David Wheeler

THAT CELT

He caught me up on sunny day
And walked close by my side,
Surprised I was to see him there,
And smilingly him eyed.
We spoke of facts, banal and brief,
Most important things,
While his laughing blue-eyed face, gave
To my feet light wings.
We walked upon the pavement grey
Not knowing where we were,
Our heads were in the clouds that day
Would this hour e'er recur?
'Twas not the sun that blinded us,
Nor traffic lights turned red,
We both did dream where this would lead,
Would that be to his bed?
Of all the crowds surrounding us,
Not one could we pick out,
Our hearts were wounded grievously,
Of that there was no doubt.
I felt his arm around my back
He drew me gently in,
His hard clean shaven cheek on mine,
I turned to kiss his skin.
I knew he'd take the other road,
How empty then I felt,
As staggering I walked away
My mind filled with that Celt.
So yet once more I wounded lie
On battlefield of love,
Does cure exist for broken heart
On Earth or Heaven above?

Mary Lefebvre

WIGAN WALLGATE

How little things have changed here down the years
That I recall; the forty years – or more –
Since, as a boy, I trainspotted, an so
Avoided shopping with my parents. Oh!
The tedium of Mother's search for clothes;
The heavy bags, on Saturdays, the droves

Of people who descended on this place,
Like summer bees about a golden hive,
Or restless ants, reluctant to submit
To weekend, or surrender to a time
Of rest; from Hindley, Abram, Aspull, Haigh,
From Shevington and Standish, on this day,

They busily proceed to bargain hunt,
Or search for special things, like rings or clocks,
Or presents for their friends, then have a meal,
Walk through the park, a chat, a cup of tea;
But me? I'll to the station, if I may,
To while away a part of shopping day.

A penny platform ticket makes me free –
For there were no place unprecipitous
Outside, no form of vantage or safe ground
From which to view or to admire this scene;
Just storage yards and tracks and granite walls,
Atop a high brick rampart – of St Paul's

I often thought, in meditative mood,
Or Abbey tall, when silence made enfold.
But when locos did combust and spit their fire,
Or sooty smoke, like fiends insane: I think
On castles, cannon and on angry siege;
Of knights and vassals, fighting for their liege.

A pigeon doth descend from perch on high!
'You daydreamer!' he seems to say . . . 'and yes,
We're still here!' I look up to his colleagues,
So cheekily aligned they make me smile!
They seem to know the Bolton train is due;
It might be full, but pickings could be few.

I think . . . on Liverpool; now there's a change –
That line has changed a lot, and change required:
At Kirkby, then by Mersey-Rail to Lime;
Still bypassing St Helens! Fancy that!
And anyone for Wavetree be stowed;
You're better off by car – on East Lancs Road!

I walk along the platform to a place
I loved and could observe the West Coast Main,
Atop a high embankment, arcing round –
To Scotland, and the north; it were as though
One stood astride the Earth's extremity,
To gaze on new dimension – past the sea!

A stellar and impressive high array,
Of all the region's finest rolling stock!
A glittering parade! A panoply!
Of diesel bound for Euston, steam for Crewe!
Of magnitude, a galaxy apart!
For trainspotters, a universe to chart!

I think . . . on Manchester, and lines that lead
To home – though we preferred to take the bus!
To our front door! Eight miles away, for as
An asteroid, or satellite, may be displaced
By work and calling, so my parents passed
Into an orbit new. And so . . . at last,

I think on Southport how we took the train,
Just me and Mum and Dad – I stayed by them –
The green of Gathurst; Parbold and its hill;
Then Appley Bridge and Burscough, Bescar Lane:
The glory of a portion of the Fylde!
So cultivated, fine and not too wild!

Oh happy days on Lord Street! Pleasureland!
Kentucky Derby! Bingo! Pitch and Putt!
Oh, railway, you were gateway to these miles!
Of happiness and joy! A thousand smiles!
And Wallgate! When I need to be consoled:
I think on thee, with reverence, now I'm old.

Alan Gore

CLOSED MINDS

The pointed finger;
The staring eyes: Tears I cried
As you walked by, muttering those words.

'There goes the one who's lost his mind,
We mustn't be unkind.'

You crossed the road from your lips,
I heard those whispers: I'm not asking for a date,
Just to be a mate.

It's your fate, giving your child a good shake,
Let's have tea, walk by the lake,
For goodness' sake, give a fella a break.

'Kate, are you having that cake or give it to your mate?'
Those slings and arrows that you throw
Won't do any good you know.

Look at the lonely crow out there in the snow.
With pointed fingers glow, you watched the wind blow.

On dark and dusty nights, eyes weren't bright,
I hated myself for I wasn't strong,
Words came out wrong.

That forgotten song played over and over in my head,
As I lay on my bed to sleep, tears flowed.

On a park bench, I sat at my wit's end,
Needed a friend, the clock on the wall ticked like a bomb,
Waiting to explode.

Words were said, misunderstandings were made,
Tempers rose, as if we were lost in a maze.

Those dreams of women teachers at school
As their voices were raised; the smacks
Would land with their hand.

So I had to stand and played in the sand,
Crying I would do, pulling out my hair too,
The torment I went through and the hurt
That I caused.

100

I cried, so sorry am I for the tormented mind,
Guess I was unkind, writing on walls, turned heads,
Closed doors.

As I walked into the room and heard
The sound of wind blowing in the trees,
The sound of birds' sings: cries of whales
A lovely breeze of fresh air.

Michael Hill

LAMENT OF THE ELDERLY

Long time dying
Forever denying
The limbo state
Their fate:

Fighting pain
Battling to stay
Sane, and understand
What life has

In store
So different from
Before:
Agony of suffering

With increasing
Medication and no
Alleviation
In spite of

Radiation.
Not crying, but
Waiting for
Long-time dying.

Lily Seibold

A BAD HAIR DAY

I am mad you know –
as mad as a hatter –
only madder than that.
I am flatter than batter
that is waiting to rise,
and that's no surprise.

My mind is warped.
It goes seeking trouble
then turns on itself
and bursts its own bubble,
thus leaving me flat . . .
and flatter than that.

I am so very low,
living yet dead.
My uselessness grows.
I'm stupidly led . . .
too futile to talk . . .
like a worm on a fork . . .

. . . or a lump of green cheese
that is mouldering fast.
I tried to think once . . .
. . . are those days past?
Like a mole on a face
I besmirch and disgrace.

I use up the fuel
that is needed elsewhere,
taking fodder from those
who are useful, who care.
Best then to go?
The answer is no!

I lack the courage
to even depart,
preferring to stay –
a target for darts –
feeling the prick,
too limp to kick.

I'm one of life's floor-cloths
under your feet –
down on the vinyl
where dirt and dust meet,
yet in the far distance
there shines a wee light –
a star in the night!

Doris Townsend

IF ONLY

I'm full of good intentions
And try to do what's right
But the daily hassles get to me
And I am all uptight
My meanest aspirations and slenderest hopes o'erboard
If only, if only I could be a little like You dear Lord
I love the things You do
And hear the things You say
That's why I want to be like You
That's what I hope and pray
What have I done to merit
Your love for such as me?
A love that triumphed over death on the cross of Calvary
Just talking to You raised me up
To walk away from my sorrow
And has given me the strength to face
Whatever comes tomorrow.

Frederick Osborne

FIRST DOODLEBUG

In that dawn, more moon than sun
Hangs a greying, wet, blue pastel sky.
With my mind I write on clouds
A name to seal the storm, still slumbering.

By the lake barked lightning rises
Slowly over eons, grasping
Forking, arcing up at birds,
That dragon? A swan in flight.
The last moment of tranquillity
On the first day of war.

My unit, to our ribs in mud
Digging trenches for men we'd never meet;
Breaking backs, callusing hands more
Used to pen than mattock
Men who aren't afraid of hard work
But only because they've never encountered it.

Our sergeant mans the heavy machine,
Steroid Stan, the orang-utan man
Sets a standard of single ply to fly
Above the Somme, his name writ large
Arrogant. The deep hum begins

In my Mickey Mouse ears
Borrowed from an eponymous friend.
The screaming starts dark,
A sky of arrows, closing fast.

Dry steam pours from ancient
Trunks, staring up at immortal
Engines,
Cutting sky.
We are not ready.

Remember the sound as we
Rattle in the back
Of rattling trucks. Homeward
Bound, pulling desperate smokes
From soiled hands.

Now deep in age
Bed-ridden, pale
I long for the stench of stagnant water
The sports hall all unroofed
To show an empty sky.

Nicolas Bowyer

SAM'S HALLOWEEN

It was upon all Hallows' Eve
When ghosts their dark, damp graves all leave
Witches and warlocks congregate
This dreadful night to celebrate

Young Sam was in the woods to poach
And on their gathering did encroach
As he saw them whirl and dance
He stood and watched as in a trance

He knew that he should run away
But something within him made him stay
And as he heard them screech and yell
Young Sam got his first glimpse of Hell

The leading warlock turned and saw him
His scowl was fearsome, dark and awesome
As two witches grabbed his arm
Sam knew that he would come to harm

Although he strove to break their clasp
They held him firmly in their grasp
And then began a game of dice
To find who would Sam sacrifice

He felt a hand upon his shoulder
And suddenly the air grew colder
A voice from somewhere he heard shout
'Come on, get up you lazy lout.'

Now when Halloween draws near
Sam still feels that twinge of fear
And on the last night of October
He goes to his bed stone cold sober.

Ian Russell

GRANDPA

His love he scattered
Over the cliffside-grey mingling in chalky white;
Grit growling – whipping –
Flinging it back in his face.
The mist of his memory clouding his view,
'Where did you go?' he whispers on the breeze,
Only the distance can be seen.
Old love of a wilted petal –
But the flower still in full bloom.
The crash of the waves beckons
Calls him to her rocky bed;
Dreaming of an endless rest,
Pain, no more.
White strands of hair, caught on the air
Knotting in wire frames;
Chequered cap wringing in his hands.
Saltwater tears fall down with the rain,
He edges towards the brink –
Two more steps to tranquillity –
Selfish desire to be with the heart.
Admiration still glowing bright
Enchantment, even now intensifying.
'Why did you leave me?' escapes in breathy sighs.
Rage brews, a thunder in his soul;
An empty sky – no gull in sight.
A faint echo of the tide, a wish for years expired.
One more step and that peace is his.
The blur recedes, his legacy surrounding
A small hand slips into his –
The warmth revives him
Back to his mortal world.
He follows blindly – back to the roadside.

Sarah Aitchison

MUMMY, MUM, MOTHER!

Mum
You're marvellous,
You're unique,
You're magical . . .

I just want you to know I love you

You deserve the world and more,
You're a superhero, my hero,
You're the one I turn to when I need a hug,
The person who wipes away my tears.

I just want you to know I love you

You know what to say when I'm feeling down,
You put up with the change in fashion.
You put up with the temper tantrums.
You have put up with more than any other mum in the world.

I just want you to know I love you

You have seen me through the worst times.
And seen me through the best times.
No matter what I do, you're always there,
But everything I do, I do it to make you proud.

So I just want you to know I love you

You're my shining star.
You're my role model.
You're my *hero.*

But most of all you're my best friend . . .
And Mum, I just want you to know I love you with all my heart and so much more.

Katy Hickey

ROPES OF COTTON

A ship sails into Liverpool
And anchors with a rope,
And the rope becomes a symbol
Of the Cotton Traders' hope.

The bales they are unloaded,
To quickly be dispatched,
To the cotton mills of Lancashire,
And its ropes with which they're lashed.

Bales reach their destination,
And quickly they are spun,
Round and round and round again,
Till threads begin to form.

Then twisted, wound and plaited
Until thick ropes are formed.

At last complete – the product
Is laid upon the ground,
When, miracle of miracles!
A circus ring is formed.

New ropes are hung from rafters,
On which acrobats can swing,
And some are used for walking,
High above the circus ring.

Other ropes are used for safety,
And assembling big tops.
Not to mention leading horses
And exotic animals of course.

From rope halters artists hang and thrill,
Twisting ropes from sheets of cotton
To climb and slide to ground again.

Landing gently in the circle of rope,
That is the circle of life,
For the circus, the spinners and their wives.

Catherine Coward

HOLD A TORCH FOR US

It is clear that in this overheated climate of ours
We can spend billions and billions, hours and hours
But we can't take the time to care for our fellow man
Maybe this summer we'll hold a torch in their hand
For the hungry, for the people who have nothing
For the kids who have dreams, to be something
To be just like their heroes up on TV
Usain Bolt or maybe Stevie G
Kids who can only idolise from what they have
And kids who would give anything to go to a match
Let's hope that with the five rings all in a guild
There's something for the future, something to build
Something to hold onto the poorest of London
I'm just putting words to it; I'm not stealing your thunder
But maybe we should be taking a time out
And start to wonder, what's this all about
These games held in the June-July sun
Maybe all the colours of the world can live as one
And just for one moment, put prejudices aside
As they cheer for each other's nation's pride
To see the taking part, nothing to lose
To see young kids on the street, something to do
I hope it's more than a mirage, someday
We may just realise what the Olympics did
To give London a will, to give us a way
Insh'allah
Insh'allah
Insh'allah.

Dan Hinton

D H LAWRENCE

Handsome of face, powerful of mind,
He wrote of love, of every kind,
With a poet's feeling, he wrote of life,
A working man's loving, sorrow and strife.
He told everything just as it was,
The cursing and the swearing, just because,
That's how folks spoke, back then,
Living and toiling they all had a yen,
For something better, D H Lawrence found it,
In his writing and family, not just a bit,
A whole lot of wonder in the fields all around,
Inspired him to put life into words and thoughts profound,
For decades his stories lay fallow in his homeland,
Not so abroad, they thought they were great, not banned,
When finally, the ban was lifted, Lady Chatterley found fame,
D H Lawrence was at the top of his game.
His tales became films and TV shows, gone was the shame,
Now he was famous, long after his death, sad to say.
Here is this portrait, painted with soil from land where he'd play,
From gardens behind his houses, where he lived and wrote,
A fitting tribute, to the man, and his work. He's got my vote!

Kenneth Jackson

THIS CROSS OF SIN

Twisted and buckled, bent to fit this form,
Held high for all to gawp 'pon this slain man.
I am but flesh of you, this Earth born.
Sit, heed this tail of sacrificial lamb.
Cry did I not for my pain, but for yours.
Revealed to me was the filth of all sin.
Over and over bore I mortal flaws.
Such was the dice played for my angel wing.
Should I be given a different choice,
Odious would be my choosing for life.
Fractured bones author quiver in my voice.
Such must I bear for your immoral vice.
In living life us mortal beings must lust
Nowt but this moment's need, we in God trust.

Jeffrey Galuidi

110

CHASING DREAMS

So often people tell me I'm chasing a fantasy
That my dream which I follow will never be
But I raise my head and ignore what they say
As they waste their lives chasing money each day.

They miss out on the beauty that's all around
And never see the miracles that can be found
They go through life with their blinkers on
Not seeing their blessings before they're gone.

It's a sad fact of life, when you live in a box
And waste precious moments checking your stocks,
And what's been acquired isn't worth the price
Of a loving heart turned to a block of ice.

I count my blessings and will chase my dreams
And won't be tied down by capitalistic regimes
I will chase my dream and I'll make it come true
It's the *most* rewarding thing in life I can do.

Monica Partridge

AN UGLY END

Alone she sits, in her room,
Surrounded by letters expressing her gloom.
Knives and razors on the floor,
Hoping her life will soon be no more.

Writing a note for whoever should care,
Her loved ones will read it if they dare.
Inside she's feeling sick and hollow,
An empty bottle of pills and tears soon follow.

She's tried before to kill her pain,
Nothing works, it comes back again.
She's growing weak and fading fast,
She must make sure she will not last.

She takes a razor and just to be sure,
Cuts her throat and falls to the floor.
She couldn't help wanting to die,
Just couldn't take the pain and lies.

Laura Smart

ASHES

If things were different
I would've taken you to Sicily.
I would've stood on the
apple-red rocks,
by the old houses you loved,
the ones with slits for windows
and ivy growing freely.
I would've watched the tide
roll in, smelled the sea salt
in the air and thought about
all the places you wanted to go.
You, the world traveller
who found his peace in Sicily,
hiking in the heat of the day
and breaking bread with the locals.
I would've held handfuls of you,
your skull, your hands, your heart,
and let them go.
But you're buried here,
in cold English soil.
Far from the city where
you wanted to grow old.
I would've taken you to Sicily
if only she'd let you go.

Erin Fitzgerald

RETURN TO THE BLUEBELL WOOD

Returning to the Bluebell Wood,
My legs on pilot now releasing my private sorrows.
For those I've loved and lost.
Within the tranquil wood sorrows soar from my very soul,
As I recall,
The years that lie behind, filling my mind
Wondering *why, why, why?*
Treasured love held invisible within my palm forever strong.
Intoxicated by the perfumed flowers, bringing comforting images, your smiles and laughing eyes.
How can there be so much beauty beneath the sky,
Yet so much beauty snatched away?
Wondering if you knew how much of me departed
When you were gone?
An endless love that blossomed like a flower.
When I leave this special place, I leave behind my sorrows clinging to the happy memories that
linger long . . .
Part of you was me, part of me was you,
No words will ever tell the grief,
An endless tapestry remains, bringing comfort and peace in the solace of the Bluebell wood,
Where once we walked hand in hand so long ago
Next spring I will return, remembering,
Weep some more, release my hidden sorrows,
Leaving behind the Bluebells
Who will never tell my tale of grief.

Liz Dicken

FACEBOOK FRIEND

When I am at home on Friday night
When Facebook is my only friend.
I thank the Lord that I can type
I thank the Lord that I can spell.

I used to wonder what we did
Before we had a phone.
I used to wonder what we did
When texting was a myth.

I marvel at this technology
Now my reference is my PC,
We think we are so clever
My Facebook friend and me.

When I am at home on Saturday night
I wonder what my friends are doing.
But then I see that just like me
The likely answer is nothing.

They posted it on Facebook you see
So now I see that just like me,
Facebook is their one true friend
Despite contacts numbering four o three.

I thank the Lord for my friend Facebook
He brings my friends from other lands,
Right to my door to sneak a peek
And to keep them close at hand.

To those contacts I met in passing
To those who have been on my travels.
I want to see your smiley pictures
I want to laugh at your wrangles.

But this is an ode to you Facebook fans
Who are daily in your seats
Keeping in touch, typing away
And live right up the street.

To you I say, I marvel at this technology
We think we are advanced.
But the way that we no longer speak
I really think is pants.

One day while sitting on your own
You'll want to use the dog and bone.
Please be patient as you will see
That suddenly no one is free.

For whilst you were typing away
A whole twelve months have gone.
Whilst waiting on your next download
Your voice has been forgotten.

I've missed when happiness
Has come and gone your way.
When you used to call me personally
It would brighten my very day.

No one can hear anxiety in typing
Nor a struggle on your screen.
For that I have to listen
But only if you speak.

So if you find you're sitting there
Remember this little ode to thee.
When Facebook is your only friend
Come and talk with me.

Charlie Burnley

ANGER DEFUSED

Take the smooth with the rough,
Be resilient and be tough.
Anger can lead to a bottomless pit.
Cross the hurdles and feel fit.
Do not be a loser, a lost cause,
Get a grip, have your own inner applause
Life has a turn and a twist,
Some pressures one does not want to exist.
Crossing the bridge takes a secure step or two
When troubled keep your head above water, do not feel blue
And, when pulled and bogged down
Do not frown
Always have courage and hope
Because you know you can cope
Cross those blues
See life, the colours, the hues,
We are all in the same boat,
So, let's keep afloat.

Kathy Carr

A CHILD'S WORTH

How precious you are little child
If rarity decides your worth
For you're unique, no other you
No perfect copy here on Earth.
But it's not so, oh little child
For mankind values not that way
For your *life's* cheap, there are plenty you
To bruise, to starve, to turn away.
A portrait by a master hand
A diamond, huge, with brilliant cut,
A massive fortune will command,
But you, my child, worth only groat.
For cross the world there are millions you
Who screech each ear-piercing cry of pain,
Neglected, hungry, beaten blue
Your hollow eyes shed tears in vain.
So can they wonder little child,
If your uniqueness finds a cause
To change it all with bomb and gun
For if you grow with brutal scars
How can you have a sense of fun?
How can for you, ought precious be
If you're not worth your daily bread
If all you've known is misery
No place for you to rest your head?
Magnanimous gestures will not change
The future for the child unborn
Without an international will,
For east and west, it is forlorn.
So press your statesmen, voters all
To turn from matters crude and wild
And let there be a clarion call
That every one's a precious child.

Matt Robson

THE ANGEL'S LAMENT

The screams of the angels will deafen
Those with the conscience to hear
As the weight of Millenia fades
So too does the weight of their fear
The sun at the crest of the morning
As vast as the lives it maintains
From the depths of the bottomless oceans
To the peaks of the highest mountains.
Mankind is engaged in this profit
No interest where nothing's to gain
Apostles of doubt with no prophet
No guide to salvation again.
As fish in the realms of the ocean
Lost in this sea of despair
While silver is lining their pockets
A Judas will always be near
First money then later comes power
'Tis the flaw of the nature of Man
To take but a little's more noble
Than to scavenge for all that he can
I firmly believe in a god
A creator of all, good and bad
Who's laid everything here at our feet
Yet we're endlessly making him sad.
There are fewer tomorrows than yesterdays
No promises written in stone
But Lord as I need you, you answer
And I know then I'm not so alone.
Lord as I need you, you answer
I know now, I'm not so alone.

Peter Walsh

QUESTIONS AND ANSWERS

'Why is the sky blue, Dad?
Why is the water wet?
Why does fire burn you?
Why does jelly set?
How do bees fly, Dad?
Who built the first jet?
Why does thunder rumble?
And fish swim into the net?
Why do babies cry, Dad?
How do I be a vet?
Why are tigers stripy?
Why can't I have a pet?
Dad, do you remember
When you and Mum first met?
Why did you have me Daddy?
Is it something you regret?
When is it my birthday?
Are you sure you won't forget?
And Daddy, please tell me why
I've got no answers yet.'

'Well let's find out my little one,
You, with me, please come
And we'll try and find some answers.
We'll go and ask your mum.'

'The sky is blue my little one,
Because God did decree
That he'd like to match it
To the colour of the sea.
Water's wet my baby
So it can get you clean,
Or be a drink to cool you,
Or make a pretty scene.
Fire burns to teach you
Sometimes you need to think.
If jelly didn't set
It would only be a drink.
If you designed a thing to fly
A bee wouldn't look so funny.
But if bees weren't like they are
We'd not have any honey.
The Wright brothers were the first to fly,
But their plane was not a jet.
So we'll get Dad to look that up

Using the Internet.
Thunder rumbles when God's hungry
And he's got an empty tum.
He makes it loud and scary
So you'll cuddle with your mum.
Fish swim into the net
So that we'll have food to eat.
Babies cry to make Dad mad,
Make him admit defeat.
Vets went to school to learn things,
Which makes them very wise.
A tiger's stripes provide him
With an excellent disguise.
You can have a pet my love,
When you can care for it,
But as you're not quite ready yet,
You'll have to wait a bit.
We had you because we wanted to,
That we wouldn't change,
Dad remembers when we met,
Though he's looking at me strange.
Finally, we come to,
The most important question yet.
It's not your birthday for a while
And I won't let Dad forget.

Lorraine Griffiths

TRAITS

People have so many traits,
Impossible to list,
Whilst some are clearly obvious,
Others can be missed.
They depend on those around us,
Which ones we have on show,
Truly linked to our emotions,
From our head down to our toe.
They rely on other's actions,
Deeds and signs of words,
Tied up within their meanings,
And how well one has heard,
Or translated from a message,
Regardless of the source,
A new communication,
Which need replies of course!
Some are filled with pleasure,
Others daggers drawn,
When things no longer go our way,
And everything's forlorn,
Our smiles can turn to scowling,
And laughter lost in groans,
As cheerful banter disappears,
When all we hear are moans!
There used to be a saying,
Which still holds true today,
For genuinely caring,
No matter what the way,
Which says that it's the actions,
Which speak louder than the words,
So are they given selflessly,
Or waiting in a terse,
Upon the tails of others,
Whose actions are sincere,
It's time those lazy jealous traits
Should really disappear!

M Wilcox

BROKEN UMBRELLAS

Those broken umbrellas,
With their spindly wings and
All colours of the rainbow limbs.
Those sorry abandoned things on
Trains and buses, peering damply
Out of litter bins.
Floating listlessly in blocked drains,
Cast aside like old sins.
Just think of all the thoughts
They sheltered, those emotions
To and fro and spinning like
Roundabouts and swings.
And the comfort of listening to
The soft rhymes and rhythms of
Hail and rain.
Those broken umbrellas with their
Sleeping life and half-forgotten names.
If only by some miracle
They could heal themselves
Flap their wings and take flight,
Those broken umbrellas,
Cocooned in their own sinister,
Magical, beautiful twilight.

Paul Jones

QUEST

Earthmen, Earthmen soaring free
From parent planet's gravity,
Cocooned in capsule's womb embrace,
Traversing unknown realms of space,
As you journey to the stars –
Beyond Jupiter and Mars,
What hidden secrets will you find
Reveal themselves to human mind?
Can there be another place
Where 'life' has formed a higher race?
Or are we the epitome
Of all creation's energy –
Living child of cosmic birth,
From embryo to 'Mother Earth'?

Beryl Andrews

CRUEL WINTER

Birds fight with fury at the hard, ice-packed ground!
Precariously pecking for some morsel of food.
The trees are bare now,
Coated with frost, their branches
Stretching like fingers
For some ray of winter sunshine.
The wind whistles through the trees
Rustling up the fallen leaves!
Barren fields stretch for miles
Like childless mothers awaiting
Their turn to give birth.
But winter is hard
On Mother nature
And she must wait a while yet
Before she can conceive.

Elizabeth Phillips Scott

THOMPSON

Thompson is my pussycat
Ginger to the hilt
Named by the Directory
Where was he built?
Many years he lived with me
A friend for life I'd say
Kept all opposition
Out of the way
Trained to be good indoors
Never any stress
Dishes for his food
Never any mess
I've had pussycats
For a long, long time
Nice purry creatures
Where's a tree to climb?
'Me, how?'

Rosemary Povey

RUN, BROTHER, RUN

Run, brother, run.
The trained hounds are after you.
Man regards you as sport.
Clowns dressed up as clowns,
high on horseback,
chase you with demonic din.
No pity or guilt for lives cruelly taken,
only pompous pleasure
and degrading glee
as they seek to outpace each other.
Run, brother, run.

Jump, sister, jump.
Let the stream be your friend.
Dodge the sharp bullet
as it stings past your head.
Hunter man is on the moors,
desiring your flesh for his table.
Deny him his selfish whim.
Today let no blood stain the heather.
You too have a right to life.
Speed safely to the cover of the forest.
Jump, sister, jump.

Hide, little one, hide,
The brutal boots will pass you by.
Keep still, do not breathe.
Beware of his snares and traps.
You do not want a death of slow pain,
only to live in the wild as born
and enjoy the changing seasons.
Man is not kind.
He interferes, and bruises the lives of others
in his ignorance and high self regard.
Hide, little one, hide.

Helen Dalgleish

JAKED ON GREEN BEERS

There's cigarette
ash
on my pillow,
And my ashtray
is an empty bottle,
Half the time I get the
ash
down the neck
the other half
I don't.
The couch and
floor
are a battleground
of cig ends and stale beer
dregs
and what makes it all the
worse
is that it's here I feel
content.
I miss meals
half the time
because I cannot be
arsed
to eat, the other half
I miss my meals
because
I have no
money for
food.
Every day I feel
like dying.
And every day
I am.
But so are you,
and so is she,
and them,
and so is every
fucking
one.

There's cigarette
ash
on my pillow,
And I feel like I'm already

dead,
But holy shit,
baby,
If this isn't
living.

Ian Critchley

AN OLD FRIEND REMEMBERED

In his '49 Ferrari which he paid for with a cheque
Drawn on the Bank of England –
He's a long way from the 'tech
I remember how he made it in 1983
But I don't think that he remembers me

He was always talking records and had the latest
Word on
Imported US labels – most I'd never heard of
He was gonna make a million – yeah, that's the
Price of fame
I doubt if he even knows my name.

We were at school together
Buddies, sort of
But he'd say things I never even thought of
The most popular boy in class
Me, the horse's arse!

He became a local deejay and sure moved with the times
I cannot give you reasons why he was making rhymes
He moved to Smoke (that's London) and lived in NW3
And probably forgot about me.

He wrote hit songs for singers, had shows in the West End
Bought a helicopter for Elton John to lend
Came home every Christmas, his family to see
And never thought at all of meeting me.

I'd see him in the local drinking gin and tonic
Delivering a wisecrack and looking supersonic
Taking out a wallet and paying carelessly
He never got a round of drinks for me

Why he should be so lucky I'll never ever know
But then he always did have much more get up and go
I'm still around and working in the bottle factory
Does he really never ever think of me?

Phillip Rowland

SEASONS

Spring
Last, lingering snow's sporadic, dirty heap
Earth is yawning off its sleep
In season vernal
The world takes on a brighter hue
Another year begins anew
The round eternal
The hedgehog and the badger, both
Sloughing off their winter sloth
While lambs are leaping
The new year's fashions are displayed
And, scattered through each woodland glade
Snowdrops are peeping.

Summer
Hazy day, lazy day, slumbering the hours away
Scarcely any balmy zephyr whispers through the trees
Butterflies and sunny skies. Softly come and distant cries
The non-stop singing of the lark; the buzzing drone of bees
Fluffy clouds and seaside crowds; raucous music . . . much too loud
Punch and Judy entertain the children on the sand
Father's knotted handkerchief gives his balding pate relief
Toddlers build sandcastles, while young love strolls hand in hand
And in the warm and dark of evening . . . marriages are planned

Autumn
Winds shunting back and forth
Blowing from the north
And every which way
Gusting, lusting after coats
Hats and scarves from throats
Each day's a mixed day
Footsteps crunch through leaves, amber and brown
More coming down
In bright profusion
Trees stand against the blast
Empty at last
In dissolution
Carpet of leaves still lingers
Dampened by foggy fingers
Merging into
Calm, but increasing cold
No need to be told . . . this heralds winter

Winter
Crisp underfoot, chill the air, the rabbit shivers in his lair
And silent all around
And iron hard the ground
Breath frosts to steam
Brittle the stream that once laughed gaily
Now hardens daily
Fields of snow imprint where Nature's prowlers go
And men and carts and all until the next obscuring fall
Those of sufficient years hand round the cup that cheers
While the tender hug the fender
Where there are chestnuts roasting
And tiny feet are toasting
Presents to buy
Advent is nigh.

Bob Lammin

THE JOURNEY

The homecoming, cheerful as I may be.
Heart warmed by companion presence.
Noticing people changed through adolescence.
News from afar to find some have gone for convalescence
How the years have taken their toll
Through hardships, we all know.
One thing remains, and is clear.
That your presence is near.
Your face is still the same.
As respected also is your name.
How thoughtful I have become.
As life's pages turn on.
Hoping friendship will be divine.
Distant views flutter by as one journeys.
But I feel like a fragile butterfly.
So give me something to grasp onto.
Like a welcome homecoming.
Nothing is measured like this.
Timeless tender hourglass.

Valerie Mathew

MY ANGEL GIRL

Linda louse was a girl who meant so much to me
For she filled my heart full of warm, tender love
And my life full of happiness and joy

Her love was so warm and tender
Her love was so soft but strong
And her love made my life worth living
On this war torn world of ours

Now that angel girl has gone from my side
And I feel so sad and alone
For my life is now filled full
Of loneliness and sorrow
And my heart is slowly turning to stone

So I'll carry on searching the world
Until I find my angel girl
And she's once more in my world
And walking by my side once more.

Donald John Tye

YOU KEEP DOING IT

You're always there
With my unfortunate hair,
Cut open with malice
And a knife right above
These sleep deprived
Bags, under dead eyes

Always always there
On a bus or at another
Sad bar serving, or with
Gormless carefree boyfriend,
On his lovely shoulder
He's always nice, and not me, isn't he?

Being the romantic (wedded man)
Puts you on yet another bus
Up against the window
Listening to the same sad songs
With yet another bottle of Scotch
Pretending not to look at her.

James Colbourne

THESE MEMORIES

All they do is haunt me
Every step I take
Every moment I'm awake
Every second I sit still
Every minute that goes by
I sigh
For these memories have been loose
Rampant
Daunting
Twisting and turning the functions of my heart
Past and present
Laughter
Time well spent
Trips I took with souls I was blessed to meet and greet
Love rides on these tides
Yet still internally
I cry
A beautiful soul I miss oh so much
That these very memories aren't even enough
I pray that one glorious day
I'll see your face again.

Tamaya Tate

SPRITE STARLING

Sprite starling.
Such a little theatrical singing and
Companioning darling.
Merrily a wooing with a high heavenward
Soprano beautiful trilling.
To my wintered weary soul in love coupling,
Such soothing company and so warmingly
Springtime,
Upon this cold bleak day,
To hear,
Arousing to see
And so naturally lovingly,
To the spirit,
Fulfilling.

Keith Newing

WONDERFUL THINGS

A baby born to love its mother,
A cute little bundle of love,
To cuddle and be there to share,
To appreciate each other,
Show the world you really care.

Flowers blooming in the field,
Colours so unique and bold,
A creation in their own right,
Smells so perfect to smell,
A new life as petals, they unfold.

Clouds like cotton wool balls,
Fluffy and white, high above,
Drifting across the mighty sky,
Sun breaks through the gaps,
Highlighting the things I love.

Love, to share with two people,
Caress the heart and give,
Perfect understanding on both behalf,
To marry, and bells ring happily,
High up in the old church steeple.

A rainbow, a spectre of colours so bold,
A crock of gold at the bottom,
Wishes and dreams,
That anyone can hope for,
Dreams of reality, so calmly to hold.

These wonderful things, I can't be without,
Parts of my life, that are so dear,
I need all these necessities,
All going on all around me,
I find them so clear.

Other things I try to cherish and show,
I really care and love,
Mother Nature at her best,
Wonderful creations to keep,
For these I really know.

Fiona Smith

ABOVE AND BELOW

I am in constant love
Heart soaked, beating love
Entranced by my surroundings
Underneath the cold sunshine
I am at peace with my being
Accepting my uncertain future
I lie upon the ground
And face the changing sky

I am in constant pain
Gut-wrenching, agonising pain
In awe of my surroundings
Beneath the daytime moon
I am at war with my emotions
Have I made the right decision?
I fall upon the warm ground
And face the music one more time.

Katie Hogan

REMEMBER ME

Remember me –
When you're all alone.
Remember me –
When you're sad and blue,
To bring you much comfort.
When you see yourself in the mirror –
You'll see me looking back at you.
Remember me –
As you light a candle,
I am your angel
And will always be your last dance.
So whisper my name – if you will . . .
In the silence of the room –
And you will hear me calling you –
Beckoning you to enter into
A magical realm you've never been to before
Together we will explore a beautiful love.

Melanie Lynn Miller

YOU AND I

Today I saw someone
That reminded me of you,
Of the time we spent together,
Although I can barely remember.
Of the smiles we would dedicate to each other,
Of the world we would mean to one another.
Of how you took care of me,
Of how you would hug me
And tell me you loved me.
Of how that would make my day,
Of how I would make your sadness go away.
Of how you seemed to be just the right size
Although you had lived a lot further than I,
And how I would remind you of Heaven
As I had just kissed it goodbye.
We had just the right amount of time,
Not a second more nor a second less,
To love everything about each other
And still miss those days,
In which you were right in the next block
And I would be able to tell you every day,
I love you.

Maria Victoria Mourad Simes

MODERN DAY COMPOSER

Mind's evoked things I'd thought I'd never think
I'm falling off the edge of my brain, I'm at my brink
Why don't I have the intuition, not light up
I've got voices in my head, 'Wake up'
Hell's bells, I'm hearing Hell's bells, they're ringing out loud in this thundery sound,
I'm bound to be bound and taped up,
As I notice the corruption before my eyes
Earth was bad but this destiny is my demise
So take me to the pleasures of her inner thighs
And take me high
Higher than the chained sky, a distant galaxy
No repercussions, nope, just love and anarchy.

Archie McDonald

GOODBYE

The ticking clocks have stopped,
The world is grey, silent,
And life will never be the same, for you are not beside us.
Only soft, slow music fills our heart,
As we remember you,
The time will slowly pass us by,
Our hearts cry out for you.
The birds have stopped their singing, and dogs have started howling.
The world will never be the same,
Our hearts are slowly pining.
But we will always see your face,
Our memories fill that void,
We're feeling so much out of place, without your guiding grace.
Goodbye is all that's left to say,
We will always miss you,
I know one day we'll meet again, till then we'll always love you.

Steve Foster

KALEIDOSCOPE OF LIFE

Ever-moving, ever-changing,
Life's pictures intensifying,
Darting 'tween broken portrayal;
Fractur'd moments of pigmental
Tone and subtle shade with fine light,
The sombre and grey with the bright.
Flashes of joy, love and hunger,
Sadness, death and even anger
Constantly moving and merging,
Configur'd pictures displaying,
Rotating, whirling through your life,
Moulding form and shape of that life.
And looking back through distant years,
You seem to be drowning in tears
In times of sorrow and grieving,
And chosen templates of living
Mirror patterns of life's matrix,
Spiralling the final helix,
The final reflection . . .

Gwendoline Douglas

AT A LOSS!

Seemingly have exhausted all subjects
That have entered my head with great fuss
Till there's nothing else for it – but –
To write of *Remus*.

Here's where there's beautiful book – manufacturing,
You can't go wrong for interest,
In whose pages there's no boredom
Remus are the best.

Yes, for a new poem, I'm at a loss,
Ideas, impressions, don't come easy
To conquer these I must waken
To be bright and breezy.

There are many rivals for me to watch
Their poems something like 'exquisite'
That when it comes to comparing my poems
Don't reach 'exhibit'.

If there's one thing in life I am proud of
It is for sure – the *Remus* books
Both for good reading and not forgetting
All their handsome looks.

When we're feeling gloomy or a little lost
And can see life is not so funny
Just pick up a *Remus* book
For special company.

Barbara Sherlow

CAREW CASTLE

Beneath a sky of azure blue,
I saw the walls of old Carew,
Standing majestic by water side,
Of Carew River where mute swans glide,

Beside the outer walls a cross,
Commemorates a tragic loss,
Meredudd seed of Hywel Dda,
Was done to death in tribal war.

Nine hundred years ago there came,
A Norman who sought wealth and fame,
He married Nest, a princess fair,
And founded a dynasty there.

FitzMaurice, FitzGerald and Carew,
From this union they grew,
And from Pembroke this gallant band,
Sailed to conquer Ireland.

Down through the ages these Geraldines,
Were honoured by both kings and queens,
In battle many bravely fought,
And gained a rich reward at court.

If stones could speak would these reveal,
The exploits of great men of steel?
Of plot and plan or joust and jest,
Pretty maid or honoured guest.

I walked from cross to vine-clad wall,
And stood inside the old great hall,
A date with destiny I kept,
To be where my ancestors slept.

Terence Leslie Iceton

A WARNING TO THE MEN OF P.O.F.

(Dedicated to 'The Triang Man')

Would I like to rest my head
Against the chest
Of a beefed-up bloke
Wearing a big hat?
And jeans?
With a big buckle on his belt?
And boots?
I'd rather play Scrabble with my brother.
Would I like to be dated?
And
Waited on?
Picked up in a flash car?
With tinted windows
And driven far?
I'd rather play Hangman with my brother.
Would I like to be pawed over?
Fawned over?
Ravished and lavished?
Half curled up smiled at?
Once in a while'd at?
I'd rather play Newmarket with my brother.
Would I like to be caressed?
By a guy with
A
Vested interest to test?
Treat me as a quest?
I'd rather play Dommies with
My brother.
Would I like to go
Dancing?
Or dining?
Bottle of wine-ing?
Would I like at all
To attend a May ball
In a taffeta gown
That sweeps on the ground?
I'd rather drink tea
And enjoy him and me
Time
With my brother.
If you want to date me
You will have to get past he

Who inspects
And protects
And who won't budge an inch.
My guardian angel
There is no other
I would trust my life
But my wonderful brother.

Kathryn Critchley-Fowler

THE OLD COACH INN

The old Coach Inn was a welcoming sight after we'd been driving for hours that night.
A log fire was burning, we quenched our thirst with a drink,
'We've plenty of spirits here,' the barman said with a wink.
'We just want a room for tonight,' we replied,
as he gave us the keys to room twenty-five.
Gathering our bags we ascended the long, dim stairway
When a floating lady passed us dressed all in grey.
We undid the door, then made sure it was locked,
As we stood hugging each other in a state of shock.
Shaking and frightened, we got into our beds,
Had we imagined it? Was it all in our heads?
The room went cold, the old inn sign rattled outside,
My friend let out a scream, her eyes wild and wide.
Someone pulled my bed covers off and flung them on the floor,
When we spotted the grey lady floating right through our door.
We both sped downstairs, having not got very far,
When we saw an old gentleman propping up the bar.
'Hello,' we chorused, 'are you booked in for the night?'
But he just vanished, giving us such a fright.
Eventually morning descended, we just had a cup of tea.
'Good morning dears,' said the barman full of glee.
'Did you have a good night? Are you feeling in the pink?
We've plenty of spirits here,' he said with a wink.

Hazell Dennison

RENASCENCE - HAIKUS

January 10th
This sad anniversary
Is a source of tears.

A white pall muffled
The footpath up to the church –
Our Moscow retreat,

Crunching through the snow.
Since then, successive seasons
Have wasted away,

Maundering like ghosts
Or abandoned dreams, drifting,
With nothing to show.

But life stirs again,
Now in the depths of winter,
Irresistibly.

Regeneration
Is the order of the day
As new shoots peep through.

Norman Bissett

GET WELL SOON

Money can bring you lots of happy times
Keeping the family members nearby
You can choose your education path wisely
Investing your wealth for future brightly
Gives you confidence to make you mind
It boots your nature with egotistic pride
Can show off in exclusive designer wear
Travel wonderful places with no lair
People will blindly worship, devoid of huff
Money can also buy you intimate love
It can provide you comfort, luxury, lifestyle
But can't buy excellent health, which can't be denied.

Farzana Nadeem

WINTER'S WHITE GLOVE

Night weans in the dawn,
As the wildlife of the countryside
Stirs, stretches out and yonder a yawn.
Bleaching rays, gleam in fingertip crowns through
Bare, bracken branches.
The warmth of the dazzling yet seducing sun
Melts the plains' frosted sheen.
Crunching of feet, cold breath
Mists of moisture trickle into dewdrops.
The naked land reveals its hues of jaded green,
Smell of pine trees perfumes the air.
The bleak landscape sits in silence,
Ice-blue sky, snowflakes flutter to a blanket of white horizon.
The sun soon fades, and the moon returns
To bathe her beauty and blanche her light into the
Bewildering, haunting foliage which shelters the wildlife
From winter's white glove.

Sian Wilkinson

FREEZE-FRAME

Here, is not the brooding
tonnage of Winchester Cathedral.
Here, the grass is not growing
fiercely, finally freed from those blades
cutting ice.

Neither here were those chalets,
Christmassed with ropes of spiced, sliced orange,
the fashioned gloops of glass,
the lavender soaps.
Not even here was that warm wait for roasted chestnuts.

But here, here was that slice
of your birthday, son,
that week you chose to spend with me
and all I see are my gloves
on your scarecrowed arms

and your smile
skating towards me.

Cassandra Scott

KAKORRHAPHIOPHOBIA

I'm fourteen,
Reading Shakespeare on the beach
Sand beneath my feet, life seems sweet,
Just me, myself and I
Not a single passer-by
So I'll read it out loud just to see how it sounds
And it is profound.
Like my feet no longer feel the ground and I have found meaning in every single syllable
I am screaming.
And now I'm shouting words into the distance,
Screaming words into existence
Not refraining any resistance,
See I know now what I want to do with my existence.
So I'll write and I'll write and I'll hold that pen tight
But there's this constant battle, this endless fight.
This fear in me that's like,
Well what if I don't get it right?
The fear of failing in what I believe in that leaves my mind and body reeling.
See I just want to get better,
Make each page wetter with every single letter that I spill from my hand through the quill.
See I have got a need to fulfil
I want to make people feel,
Strip it down and make it real, break that seal.
I want to get on stage and rain my parade and not be afraid,
Stay up for nights and days just writing
Instead of fighting writing, afraid of getting it wrong
This has been my song for far too long.
See I'll get lost and I'll forget where I belong
But at times we all go wrong
It's all about staying headstrong.
See you'll know when it works,
When your whole body is shaking
When it seems like the world is trembling and awakening
When you know that the future,
Is there for the making.
So let's stop deliberating and start creating
The whole world is out there just waiting, it's yours for the taking,
So let's get lost in a maze and make it to the middle
Make sense out of every single riddle.
See it's not given to you on a plate,
You have got to build it up slate by slate before it's too little,
Too late.
So don't just get in a state and let time go to waste
Go try something new,

Unfold a story that you never knew,
See there is always something more to learn and millions of lefts to turn.
I mean our lives are not scripted so don't follow the screenplay,
You've got to seize it while you can before you start to decay
See I am trying my hardest to find the right way
But I'm still fighting the fear that is keeping me here.
So fast forward four years
And I'm standing on stage for the first time
About to tell my first rhyme,
And as I take the mic in hand
In feel the blood rush to my face at such a rapid pace
And without haste my cheeks go from pale to pink with one single wink,
So I blink and let myself sink,
Back into me and not the sea of faces staring back at me
Not knowing what to expect as I begin to project,
And one minute in it feels like there's fire underneath my skin
Like there's something awakening within,
Like my whole life is only just about to begin.
And now I'm turning my curses into verses at the flick of a page
See I have learnt a lot for my young age
But it's still taken me so long to step that stage.
But I have broken the fear now
Just to be standing right her now
And it all seems clear now,
See fear is just a state of mind
You have got to take that risk to see what you can find.

Jessie Durrant

THE VOICE OF LOVE

Love has a voice that is soft and gentle,
Smooth as butter and sweeter than honey.
Love is pure, true and kind,
Captivating our hearts and minds.

Love is sweet. It never has a bitter taste,
Love is not harsh and rude but is full of grace.
It flows like a stream in the valley
And gives no place to hate or folly.

Love is like a shining light,
It can make the bleakest countenance bright.
It has within, a magic wand,
That can give the meanest heart a song.

Love has its fire in winter's coldest hour.
The warmth of love can always be ours.
Hold on to love. Don't let it go.
A heart of love is a heart to know.

S G Grizzle

THE THINKER

Sits down, drums his fingers on the table
A few years ago smoke would have filled the air,
The pub's all clear now, conditioned in fact
Apart from the local alcoholic with his diseased throat hack

The modern day thinker, head in his hands
Struggling with issues he fails to understand
Thoughts swim round his head like bubbles in his beer
The next step in life, taken with great fear

There's no war to fight, or lose friends in
Or hunt for his next meal, or scavenge in the dustbin.
His problems are much darker and shady . . .
This modern day thinker has to go home to a modern day lady.

Iain Massingham

THE BEACH

Long marrieds dozing in their deckchairs
Nothing more to say

Young foreplayers frolicking in the sand
Longing for darkness

Old maids and widows walking joyfully
Free of men

Junior crabbers catching clawed crustations
Squealing when they nip

Gnarled ex mariners' eyes searching the horizon
Where once they used to sail

Grandads glancing at bare-bosomed eye candy
Now alas unavailable

Toddlers dropping ice cream on their mums and tums
Ignoring the scoldings

Dogs scampering and worse along the seafront
Banned from the sand

Kite fliers causing chaos when they crash
Into people and picnics

Anglers casting and winding in
Catching nothing

Tiddlers strapped in their plastic-screened pushchairs
Protected from everything

Suddenly the sun dips and the beach is bare
Tea time.

John Anstice Brown

THE VISITOR

I had a little visitor
It was a little mouse,
Running around and peering in
From just outside my house.
It ran up to the patio door
And stretched till it could see,
Me busy at the ironing board
Dog watching carefully.

Mouse climbed onto the window sill
And into the kitchen peeped,
Then quickly moving onwards
To the garden chair it leaped.
A brick was lying on that chair
The kind with holes right through,
So Mouse decided to have a game
Weaving in and out of view.

A barrel with a lid on
Was next to be explored,
With the water settled on the lid
He carefully washed his paws.
Then he decided to have a climb
So to honeysuckle he sped,
Climbing up to the top of the wall
Till he fell and banged his head.

After a second he was off again
Back to play once more,
Playing a game of hide-and-seek
In a pot next to the door.
Running underneath the sink
He'd pop up the pipe overflow,
Stopping every now and again
To see which way to go.

Then the dog began to bark
The mouse, it fled in fright,
Straight across the yard it ran
Taking hasty flight.
Up onto the coal bunker
It climbed, it did not wait,
Before it dropped upon the ground
And out below the gate.

I must confess that the little mouse
Was as cute as cute could be,
And I did enjoy his antics
As I watched him happily.
But if he had been inside my house
The story would be changed,
For I must confess they terrify me
And leave me quite deranged.

Dot Young

STILL BLUE

Sometimes I wish that I would never
Have left home so early.
Sometimes I wish that I would have
Stayed in foster care.
Now I'm in yours . . .
You are my worst enemy.
I wish you never begged friends with me.
The first sign was madness.
The second just paranoia.
I wish it wasn't.
Ignored the symptom, caught like a disease.
I'm innocent although on the contrary,
I was proved wrong.
I made that decision.
Now moving along.
Going through like an appeal,
Patience is still a virtue.
Still blue.

Aaron Noel

UNA ALMA LINDA - A BEAUTIFUL SOUL

I wished upon so many stars
Yet my wishes have not come true
'What have you wished for?'
A voice asks from afar,
'I wished for peace in this world in turmoil,
Because of money, nuclear power and black oil.'
'And what else?' the voice continues.
'I wished for my dear ones to have
Health, wealth, honesty
And a purpose-filled future –
And for the people I know
And the ones I know not,
Who are part of the human race,
To understand and tolerate each other
And for animals and plants to be
Spared from extinction
And for our planet to survive
For billions more years.'
'And for you?' the voice whispers
While fading away –
'What have you asked for?'
'I lost count of how many things
Would make me happier than I am.
Perhaps I had at least one wish
Which came true:
My soul is clean, my conscience clear,
My being adapts to any situation
And I'm able to take everything in my stride,
With strength and with a smile.'
The voice sounds distant now, I can barely hear,
'Contentment,' it says.
'That's all it takes to have a happy life!'

Noris D'Achille

BEACHCOMBER

Running breathless along the beach
With the crashing waves breaking
Still fierce from the storm
Which had been so wrecking.

It was sad to think of lost lives
And see flotsom galore
But thrilling to discover
The many items 'thrown' ashore.

The news was spreading very fast
So I raced along with jacket flying
No time to do up zips or buttons –
Plenty of booty without trying.

What a piece of luck – a basket
Constructed of wicker twisted well;
I plucked it eagerly out of the sea
And leapt back quickly from the swell.

Into my trophy container
I threw in many, many things unsold
Including cups, saucers, bowls and plates
All of plastic but 'good as gold'!

Caroline A Carson

ONLY TIME WILL TELL

Where will I be in five years' time, it's difficult to think
What makes me tick, what is my goal,
Aspirations, hopes and dreams.
Although there is no longer smog,
I find it hard to see – obstacles are in my way
Everything
I'll start tomorrow, nothing for today.
When will I wake up and see that this is my only chance to be . . .
Don't leave for tomorrow what you could do today,
Why can't I get my act together and wake up from this trance
I want to start the piano, I want to learn to dance.
I want to speak in different tongues . . .
Go out and have a life.
Where will I be in five years' time, it's difficult to think . . .
I don't even know where I am today or where I was last week.

Josephine Marle de Cera

CORY MONTEITH: THE STAR

He really is like a star to me,
Every time he appears on my TV,
Singing and dancing are what he does best,
He literally has no time to rest.

He stars in the hit TV show 'Glee',
Which I watch every single week.
The boy he plays, his name is Finn Hudson,
You should see how many competitions he's won!

He's worked hard to get to where he is now,
He should really take a bow!
He's worked in so many different jobs in his younger days,
He's a superstar, they all say!

He's a very humble and down to earth man,
Who really believes he can,
Achieve everything he sets out to do,
But remember, he's just a regular person, like me and you!

The actor's name is Cory Monteith
And he was born in the country of Canada, you see.
He's my idol as he is a talented man who
Is a star in his own right.
His star really does shine very bright!

Michaela Beth Gibson

LOVE

Looking out the windows to life
I captured your image
You posed for my attention
Turning smiles into laughter
Words formed a story in the making
Writing that first chapter
Two authors sharing pages
Bound by the fabric of affection
Sipping from the golden cup of Eros
Cupid spiked the brew
Tasting fruits from the garden of Eden
Leaving me drunk within your presence
Rippling the circle of our existence
We swam depths of new meaning
Drowning the boundaries of ego
You made me forget myself.

Michael Fields

FATHER'S DAY

Too old to be longing for a father
Too young to be acting like a martyr
What I feel I wouldn't wish upon another
One day I'll have a son who will have a brother
And when they're old they'll both agree with each other
That they were extrememly lucky to have such a good father.

Sammy Yoka Lindo Engele

TO LEE

A pain that lasts a lifetime,
The hurt, that never healed,
A hope, that dies each day it lives,
Heart broken, never sealed.
A half, that's left, unable to breathe,
Without being a whole,
A body, lives on, in darkness,
That day you took my soul,
A heart that beats though broken,
A life, that it can't feel,
Every beat, it has no meaning,
Of a loss, that it can't heal,
A bond you made unbreakable,
A whole, that's me and you,
To believe the unbelievable,
A dream, I wished, come true.
How did you hear me call you?
You heard all my cries,
To cross two worlds to heal me,
To dry my empty eyes,
Although I cannot see you,
I feel you in my heart,
A whole, I feel completely,
Now, forever start.

Kerry Mclean

FIGHTING FOR PEACE

Modern war so distant and yet so near
Beamed in daily as background noise.
War reporters share news via video phone,
Coffins draped in flags returning home.

Not how soldiers should get back home
People stand along the road and weep
Old men stand proud and sad
For someone's brother and someone's dad.

Their war was on the home front
Families died in bomb-crushed houses
The soldiers just across the sea
Fighting men just like you and me.

For freedom they tell us, men must fight
For freedom and for what is right
For what is freedom without the fear,
Of losing everything we hold dear?

Cities destroyed, spirits blighted
Endured so that wrongs are righted
Fighting for peace seems so insane
Yet we do it time and time again.

When can the world live in peace?
When will war be over?
When can all wars end?
When Man is Man's best friend.

Diane Drinkwater

FOR HECKERT

So long have I waited to hold you,
That my heart has just one beat.
Wrap me in your eyes,
And I might wait there when you blink.
A serpent's voice that you lie,
But I'd stalk those words to Hell.
A God that declares me mad,
But He made you what
Beauty is to my words.
Lo, what songs might I sing,
After you stole my very breath?
This war with myself can flatline,
For the half drunk bottle we might win.
And I would steal back the stolen,
If you would but take it from these hands,
Wither beside God's final rose,
If you would just rise there
Instead.
Is it that your eyes are green,
Or do my dreams ignite in my palm?
This empty road, my mind,
Petals of an unsung soul
Trapped in a misted jar.
And still my heart strings play for you,
This cage where I might be free.
You're the past that became
My present,
And beneath the paper
There lies my future
Ah, there are a thousand stars at night,
And in my dreams,
They paint your face
And I'd take your nightmares
For myself,
For only then might I find sleep.
The laughter to my joke,
The forgiveness to my sins.
I remain a single string,
To a puppet master
That no longer exists.

Chris Glover

THE DENTIST CHAIR

Why is it we despair at the dentist chair?
Tooth extraction is a traumatic affair
We would rather suffer the ache and pain
Opening our mouth we see no gain

The probe approaches to dig and display
The mirror in support to show decay
'That needs attention,' the dentist says
'I will drill out a cavity, there will be no pain
Fill the tooth so it can remain.'

Modern technology offers some respite
Gas and ether a past delight
We now get the needle, a couple of jabs
Numbs your gum till you feel quite drab

Out comes a tooth with an almighty grab
Root and canal, a large gap
Bags of padding so gums won't flap
Replacements cost one hell of a wrap

The crown and the bridge are not cheap either
Need constant attention, a bit of a mither
Or full set of dentures, a master sculpture
Help you become a masticate muncher

Hygienist will say there is a way
To avoid the chair and stay away
It's to eat the fruit not sugar and candy
It keeps your teeth all strong and dandy

This way you will suffer less pain and worry
And escape the chair in one quick flurry
So follow the advice and you will be fine
The dentist chair will be in decline.

Michael Entwistle

WHAT IS LIFE?

Exactly what is life?
It's a challenge,
A goal, reality,
And a presence.

Life is something we live,
Put on Earth to do one thing,
Make the most of what we have,
That's what life is.

We have been put here,
Given some talents,
To make life worth the most,
And achieve our dreams.

Life isn't supposed to end,
In an accident or by chance,
Our life ends,
When we can give no more.

No one should decide when we pass away,
Grant us that dream,
We are here to achieve a goal,
Whatever way we can reach it.

Car crashes, accidents and murders,
They shouldn't happen,
Why spoil our life by doing something stupid,
What does our life mean?

To me it means doing what you can to succeed,
To make the most of what's around you,
Don't judge and don't hate,
Don't be a fool and make mistakes.

No one should argue,
We should all get along,
One day the people we argued with,
Are gone and we never said goodbye.

No one should judge us,
We can only do our best,
For some people we have more than others,
We shouldn't take that to heart.

Why can't everyone get along?
Be there for each other,
Help where we can,
Be there when we can.

Black or white,
There is no difference,
We are human,
Nothing more, nothing less.

Some can be quicker than others,
At solving a certain task,
But some people laugh at us,
If we have a question to ask.

We aren't different,
We all deserve what we can,
Some just want to be greedy,
And won't help when asked to.

What is life exactly?
We live it, we see it,
We are it, we breathe it,
We need it, we heed it.

Life to me is simple,
It's a task we share,
Make the most of what you can,
Before it's too late.

Don't have arguments,
And leave loved ones at bay,
We all need someone close,
Regardless of the day.

Don't be a meanie,
Help when you can,
One day roles can be reversed,
And you're stuck without a plan.

Life is our challenge,
The goal we have been set,
No matter what you do in life,
Never give up on it yet.

Darran Ganter

STANDING IN THE UNEMPLOYMENT LINE

I am running out of time. I am losing my mind.
Standing in this unemployment line. The electric
Bill is due, no I am not fine! I don't have a dime.
The refrigerator's empty. Bill collectors are

Threatening to come and get me. No one has any
Patience or sympathy. Imagine living in a house
With children with no electricity.

I flip through the newspaper's classified pages,
Knowing that whatever I receive will be of the
Lowest wages. The government is breaking down
Our earned benefits into stages. I feel weightless
In a world of heavy burdens. Does my senator
Or congressman even know that I'm hurting?

Fumbling through the lint in my pocket. I am

The target of judgmental eyes. Having no money
Leaves me paralysed. What kind of plan can
These politicians devise? Factory after factory
Continue to downsize. Escaping taxes as they
Move to Mexico, telling their former employees
Lies.

I stand behind professors, teachers, carpenters,

Dishwashers, social workers time after time. I am
Feeling defeated in this unemployment line.

Christopher D Sims

A HOME OF OUR OWN

Today is the day,
I can hardly breathe.
It's ten years ago since
We walked up the aisle,
With hope in our hearts
And a dream of a
Home of our own.
We both worked hard,
In jobs we loved;
Day and night we laboured,
Tom, in his office of law,
Me in the theatre of dreams,
Dreams of people who sit
And watch the play unfold,
In a theatre dark and still,
As onto the stage
He steps, a man
You once saw in a film,
But now, there he is
As real as you and me.
That's my job, making people's dreams come true,
Yes, Tom and I have jobs,
That pay us well, and we've
Saved all our married lives.
Still it has taken ten long years,
So as I moved towards
My first dream home, I stopped
To think, how can others
After a lifetime of work,
With jobs less fortunate
Than us, ever buy a home
Of their own?
But today is our day,
Tom will carry me over the
Threshold of our first home,
We will fill with love
In the years to come.

Audrey Allen

A JUNGLE CHRISTMAS

'It's only a week till next Christmas,' said a lion to a passing gazelle.
'Let's get together the apes and the chimps and all of the others as well.'
So the next day they all got together to arrange a big Christmas do
And the lion said to the zebra, 'I promise not to eat you.'
The hyena burst into laughter till he shook like a plate full of jelly.
Till a snake hissed, 'Be quiet, I don't think it's funny to end up in somebody's belly.'
'Right,' said a bat, 'that settles that, let's decide on what we shall eat.'
When a plump fallow deer who was standing quite near, said, 'I vote we forget about meat.'
'Hear, hear,' said the pigs, 'we can eat nuts and figs with all sorts of fruit to follow.'
'With rice and bananas, some pears and sultanas. We'll start getting ready tomorrow.'
'Hang on,' said a chimp, who walked with a limp, 'I do hope it isn't too far.'
When a giraffe who was there stuck his nose in the air and said, 'Why not hire a car?'
'Don't be a goon,' said a cross-eyed baboon, searching for fleas in his hair.
'Have a word with a bird, they're friendly I've heard. I'm sure that they'll fly you there.'
So they all went away and the very next day started to gather the feast.
'There are so many coming,' said a bird that was humming. 'There must be a hundred at least.'
The chimps picked some grapes, helped by the apes, which the elephants turned into wine.
But as each used their trunk they finished up drunk and cried while they sang 'Auld Lang Syne'.
Well, on Christmas Eve they couldn't believe that so many animals had come.
The cross-eyed baboon sang out of tune and the ape beat its chest like a drum.
A pair of field mice, who sang very nice, sang 'Come All Ye Faithful' so sweet,
That the hippos all sighed and a little chimp cried, while an ape wiped his eyes with his feet.
A group of gazelles did a dance with some veils and a hippo did conjuring tricks
And a young turkey hen said, 'Look at this then,' and produced half-a-dozen small chicks.
Then a rather long snake made a mistake while doing a strange sort of dance.
It wasn't till later said an old alligator, 'The rabbits are all in a trance.'
Then high on a bough screeched the wise owl, 'Stop this at once, this is shocking.
You heard what I said, now all go to bed and remember to hang up your stocking.'
The night passed away and on Christmas Day the animals woke with delight,
As they shouted with glee, it was easy to see that Santa had come in the night.
The owl said, 'O look, he's left me a book,' and the hippos each had a new flute
And the chimp looked so grand as they all watched him stand, dressed in a real cowboy's suit.
The apes were quite glad when they saw what they had. A present that everyone likes.
They were cheered as they passed, going quite fast, each on their new racing bikes.
There was such a great noise as they played with their toys with chatter and screeching and squeals,
With guns going bang and carols they sang, and the swish of the apes on their wheels.
Suddenly Bat shouted, 'What's that?' and everyone listened to see.
Then everyone heard, with a sob on each word, 'Santa left nothing for me.'
They all gathered round and there on the ground sat a bear cub with tears in her eyes,
She sobbed, 'I've been good and behaved as I should and I'm sure that I never told lies.
But as you can see, he left nothing for me and I can't find my mum or my dad.'
They started to sigh and some had a cry and everyone felt really sad,
At the back of the crowd a voice shouted loud, 'Has anyone here seen our child?'

They all turned to stare, it was Mum and Dad Bear, then everyone went really wild,
Pushing their way to where bear cub lay, her hands tightly crossed on her tummy,
She rubbed both her eyes and screamed with surprise, 'That's my daddy and mummy.'
Holding her near, her mummy said, 'Dear, there, there you silly young cub,
Now stop crying please and give me a squeeze,' and they both enjoyed a bear hug.
'What about me?' said Mr Bear, 'you can spare me a kiss I suppose?'
'Of course I can, Dad, I'm so very glad,' and she kissed him three times on the nose.
'I'm sorry we left, we weren't very long but we had to go home for your gift.
Although it's not far, we haven't a car, so we had to rely on a lift.
It's all over now so let's dry your eyes, it's Christmas, a time to be jolly
And Santa has been and you have your dream, a lovely new pram and a dolly.'
Well, they all gave a cheer and drank ginger beer and everyone pulled Christmas crackers,
The hyenas laughed and the monkeys went daft and of course, all the ducklings went quackers.
They hung paper chains and played lots of games, especially of course snakes and ladders,
They climbed up the trees with considerable ease and slid down again using adders.
Well, the party went on till the sunlight had gone and they all had a wonderful day,
When a weasel said, 'Blow, it's a long time to go, next Christmas is so far away.'
Then an elephant said, 'I'm ready for bed and cheer up, be happy and hearty.
I'll give you a treat, it's my birthday next week and you're all coming round to my party.'

R C Clark

THE MEDIATOR IS MUTE

Who is stuffed with victory?
None except the insane,
All are lost in a cauldron of bitterness,
Misunderstanding, hate and blame.
Fanatic versus idealist
The timeless gladiators
Who wipe their feet in blood.
Defeated is the realist,
The mediator is mute it seems
His options withered away.
A weaver of dreams,
Left for another day
Despite all the pleading
The hounds of war still bark.
Is there a future? Sure,
But that figure has blood in his hair
And many more years of bleeding.

Colin Burnell

TWO PHOTOGRAPHS

How many of them?
Hundreds I suppose,
All looking up
At the camera above.

Most wearing flat caps,
Some wearing boaters,
A few wearing bowlers,
Just ordinary blokes.

The caption says,
The young men of August,
British recruits waiting
For their pay.

Another photograph almost the same,
Most men wearing boaters,
A few wearing bowlers,
Not so many wearing flat caps.

The caption says,
In Berlin, a German
Officer reads out the
Kaiser's orders.

Two photographs dated August 1914,
Almost the same,
One taken in London
One in Berlin.

I suppose it was not long
Before they were wearing
Helmets of steel and uniforms
Of a different design.

And that they did
What they had never
Thought that they would ever do
Nor ever dreamt it.

And in the years that followed,
Those that survived that martyrdom
Saw their wasted sacrifice
Some twenty years on.

I cannot help but feel sad
Looking at two photographs
Knowing with hindsight that for
Some of them violent death came.

It is their innocence
Of what was coming
That touches me the most.

Robert Lockett

NIGHT SKY

I stand alone
Gazing into the night sky
Visualising my parents
In my mind's eye.

Along with my true friends
And companions
I've lost and put to rest.

Knowing in my heart
It's all for the best
But in my thoughts
I can't let go.

They gave me life and protection
I love them so,
Each shining star
Looking down on me
Are friends and companions
And much loved family.

Phil Clark

MOODY TRUDY

It was bad enough trying to sleep last night with thoughts of what was to come
But at 7am, local time, on a Saturday morning in May (it's too much)
Is simply mind-destroying 'cause I feel I'm dying?
While trying to hold myself together
But I hear my heart beating and can see a spiderweb above the mirror,
The pulse in my neck intensifies with every brushstroke over my now tender gums
And the sensation under my fingernails is repeated through the bruise on my shin that I thought
had gone

Down in the kitchen I can't face food and it's hard just to sip the orange juice
But Mum gives me one of those (far too much)
I've been stewing down here since 6am looks
As my trembling hand lifts a slice of her cremated toast . . .
Then as I feel my heart beating I can see a spider on the floor,
The pulse in my neck intensifies with every stride it takes
And the sensation under my fingernails is repeated through the bruise on my shin that I thought
had gone

Oh please wake up Dad, it's going on 8am local time
Oh, sorry Mum, I just can't eat a thing (it's far too much)
And her wrath is complete as she screams at me while holding my plate over the dog's bowl
'You can't play on an empty stomach darling, because if you faint they might think it's Dad's
aftershave.'
Ah, please don't mention cheap scent, you're turning my belly
And what with his hair gel lingering in the hall, I feel like kicking that dog . . .
Now I feel my heart beating as I see that spider getting closer,
The pulse in my neck intensifies with every slurp the dog makes across its gums
And the sensation under my fingernails is repeated through the bruise on my shin that I thought
had gone

At last Dad comes to breakfast and I could swear he had a bald patch last week?
Mum starts going on at him about me as he starts to shake his head (but not too much)
Dad moans, 'You're getting too worked up, dear, and that isn't good for you.'
I just go into a trance and block out everything
And looking at the TV I can't even see it
'Cause I only have thoughts for me which become locked into my stare . . .
Now I feel my heart beating as the dog side-steps that spider,
The pulse in my neck intensifies with every click of the clock hand
And the sensation under my fingernails is repeated through the bruise on my shin that I thought
had gone

Even though I want to win the cup today, I know I will; fail as I always do!
It's perplexing why I'm too scared to play my best (so very much)
And how I wish it was all over so I can go back to living an ordinary life,
Everyone tells me I'm good but I don't feel I really am
Because all those other players don't get nervous

Even though they are not that good and appear uglier than me!
But maybe this game's just for mugs after all?
Because I feel my heart beating as I head to the car,
The pulse in my neck intensifies with every step I take
And the sensation under my fingernails is repeated through the bruise on my shin that I thought had gone.

Thomas McDougall

KNOCKING ON HEAVEN'S BACK DOOR

A singing dancing
VIP
Someone I'd seen
A face on the
Telly

Standing right next to me
Waiting in line
A slow-moving queue
One at a
Time

Hoping to find
Their sins forgiven
And their names on a list
To the Kingdom of
Heaven.

James Tierney

THE DECORATIVE SPADE

Once there was a spade,
A spade that wouldn't dig.
One boggles why a spade was made
That wouldn't dig a fig.

Tu-whit, tu-whoo,
The puzzle being a hard 'un
One questions what a spade might do
When useless in the garden.

No stranger an implement there ever could be,
An enigma regarding its purpose,
A sort of appendix amongst toolery
Baffling and seemingly worthless.

Well, everyone and his donkey were drawn to the spade,
Quite categorically it wouldn't do a hoot.
Cement unmixed, waiting to be made,
Bricklaying work up the shoot.

Holes still waiting to be dug,
(a somewhat contradiction)
All digging work left down the plug,
You'd think this poem fiction.

There was of course a comical side
For those who weren't delayed
Some laughed so much they almost cried
And all because of a spade.

'Why won't it dig?' those 'holers' asked
'Whyever did it come to be made?
A useless object for manual tasks,
What a silly spade.'

And thus it leaned against the wall,
A topic of conversation.
It appeared to be really no use at all
Except perhaps as decoration.

Peter Terence Ridgway

LIFE

I wished once upon a time for you,
My handsome Prince Charming.
A knight in slightly dented armour
With something unique about your smile
And how I slipped into your arms . . .

Somehow your voice ensnared me,
Bound me in fallen, spinning words
Until they dragged me down
And I felt soil clog my nose and mouth . . .

Only silence met screams
Which clawed their way out.
My hands twisted in the fingers of sisters
Seeking what little comfort
Those who've been ignored will give.

Tears fell quiet to dry on stained cheeks
As your voice held soft and sweet
Your lullaby that stunted spades and picks
Whose bodies swung to break your chains.

The key locked away in my own chest,
I too fearful to beak it open or test,
If I could fix the lock once you were gone
Repair the damage wrought,
Stumble, perhaps walk, run on.

Someone waited by the grave
Offered their heart for shattered shard.

I tore my nails to crack rocky ground
Dragged myself from you burial mound.
And shunned the help of outstretched hands,
Had to scramble upon scraped knees
But at least what drove me forward was me.

If I stop to rest a bit,
Exhausted, the shards of crystal will drop and chip
Scattered, lost and missing a piece.
Absence is always heavier to carry.

Someone waited by the grave . . .
Soon I'll be close enough to see his face.

Carol Forrester

ASPERITY

A warrior's life was chosen for me,
To fight in battles across the seas.
To see the bloodshed and spill no tears,
But alone at night I dream my fears.

Night falls swift, our next battle draws near
As flaming arrows swarm skies once clear
Around me the screams of our horses' distress
And taunts are heard from the enemy fortress

The flying death from the trebuchet,
Helps us break the siege and forge our way.
I hear the clashes of shield and steel,
As I run men through with a warrior's zeal.

Rotting corpses litter the field,
How many fell to this sword I wield?
Our spears protruding from enemy chests,
Bitter testament that our side fought best.

Their dead eyes are staring up at me,
Has our justice truly set them free?
Should I be rejoicing in their downfall,
Or sit and weep at the carrion's call?

As I begin to sicken of this warrior's life,
I yearn for peace and to take a wife.
The harshness of conflict has taken its toll,
The screams of the dying burden my soul.

Chris Janes

SING A SONG OF BUSINESS

Sing a song of business
And the credit crunch
Shares are losing value
Millions before lunch

Now the debt is owing
Can it be paid back?
What can get the economy
Growing and back on track?

Lord King was in the bank
Quantitatively easing money
The rich were in their mansions
Eating caviar and honey

The Euro was in the basement
Currencies were being sold
Investors were all panicking
And buying up the gold

Millions out of work
The high street shops are empty
But bankers still get their bonuses
And live a life of plenty

The rich are getting richer
The poor remain the poor
Is the capitalist system
Working anymore?

Andrew Fisher

BOTALLACK MINE

Today I walked the cliffs beside Botallack Mine
The sky was grey and sullen and the wind
Moaned on the outcrops that to seaward lay
A curlew cried its mournful lost lament,
It seemed to be the fitting ending to a winter's day.
There to the right and to the left lichen-clad stone and moss
And sheep that cropped at the meagre pasture
Paused and looked up with vacant, staring gaze.
Far up in clouds of pending dusk
A chough observed and circled in the haze.
Old ruined mineworks like black scaffolds by a copper sea,
What subterranean secrets do you hold?
What labyrinth of galleries moan and sigh
Beneath the crush of rock, the vent of sea,
The vaults where long gone miners worked and died?
Across the ocean long ago, the foreign traders came
To trade with silks and gold for Cornish tin,
In clefts of rocks, in caves beside the sea
Both saint and hermit made their dwelling place
And brought a message that would set men free
But as I looked, a wave in sunder tore upon the rocks
Dashed up around the headland where I stood
Scattering a million drops of salty spray,
The twilight deepened on Botallack Mine
It seemed to be a fitting ending to a winter's day.

Frances M Searle

WONDROUS BUTTERFLY

Wondrous butterfly,
You flutter in the fields' wide open space,
In spring and summer's wondrous place,
Where the scarlet-red poppies' petals
Catch the wind that blows,
Where the wheat grows,
You flutter around with a bird's eye view,
You love the sweet-scented lavender
And the cornflower-blue,
You flutter in the woodlands
Where the bluebells stretch far and wide,
Like the blue seas,
You love to listen to the bluebells tinkle
In the summer breeze,
You flutter in gardens
Where everything was once so forlorn.
Now nature is smiling,
The robin, blackbird, and starling,
You flutter near a peaceful stream,
As the warm sun shines bright,
In the long summer eves
That turn to night.
You flutter in the meadows sweet,
Where the fragrant flowers grow,
You love to say hello
To the skylark, swift and swallow,
You than rest on a flower,
Dreaming of tomorrow.

Joanna Maria John

MOTHER NATURE

In days of old,
For the common cold
And other ills
There were no pills.

So folk relied
On what plants supplied
Such as lemon balm
To keep one calm.

Rosemary and thyme
Lavender – sublime!
For scenting a room –
And lifting gloom!

Plants from the field
With their welcome yield
Helped cure all ills –
There were no pills.

Kathleen White

GOD'S GIFT

God gave me England
As the land of my birth
England gave me my homeland
The best there is on Earth
Surrounded as we find ourselves
By the best of British
Not the kind to let you down
When things are getting skittish
We have the best of neighbours
With the Irish, Welsh and Scots
There are those who would undo us
With their dark and devious plots
Once more must we rally
In defence of all who are free
And stand to defend
God's greatest gift
The gift of liberty.

B D Vissian

RAIN

How I love the falling rain,
Heaven's way of watering flowers,
I could sit and watch for hours
The falling rain.

How I love the April showers
Filling up the tinkling rills,
Kissing golden daffodils,
Coaxing life from sleepy seeds,
Decking grass with diamond beads,
The April showers.

How I love the stormy rain,
The fury of the thunder crash,
The beauty of the lightning flash,
Then blue-black skies release their all
Like some gigantic waterfall,
The stormy rain.

How I love the summer rain,
Cool and fresh and smelling sweet,
Damping down the sweaty heat,
Dancing free from fluffy clouds,
Laying dust, dispersing crowds,
The summer rain.

How I love the drizzling rain,
With choking fingers cold and clammy,
It gets in every nook and cranny,
With dull grey drapes it blots the view,
Unceasing, creeping, seeping through.
The drizzling rain.

How I love the steady rain,
Mother Nature's washing day,
Rinsing dirt and germs away,
Sluicing streets and flushing drains,
Swilling mountains, swabbing plains,
The steady rain.

How I love the falling rain,
Heaven's drink for thirsty earth,
Could gold or silver match the worth
Of falling rain?

Ken Birch

MY HUBBY

The nights are long and lonely
Without you, my dearest heart,
We were soulmates forever
And never to drift apart
I never heard you grumble
When life grew tedious
You always had a smile for everyone
Although you were suffering,
You are always with me,
When I feel down at heart
The loss I feel for you my dear
Is so hard to bear
Now we are far apart
Although I cannot see you
I can feel your presence
Around me all the time
Sweet memories of times gone by
Still linger in my heart
Your handsome face
Your laughing eyes
The tenderness in your smile
I feel so lucky to have known you
For such a short while
Your kind heart and gay laughter
Always filled my heart with joy
I will always love you, my dear
Although we are so far apart
Time goes by so quickly
The years just roll away
Each day I look at your photograph
To help me through the day
I'm sure your lips move
And tell me
All the things I want to hear
'I will always love you, my dear
Even though I am not there.'

Doreen Brialey

CLAIRE

Claire, don't give me that stare
Pull up a chair
Sit down over there
Park your derrière
Don't touch my éclair
From the cake stall in the market square
If you're hungry, have a pear
You should lose some weight, yeah
But for you, willpower is rare
Do you have something to declare?
Don't think I'm not aware
I know you're having an affair
I thought we were a pair
I don't know how you dare
I'm trying not to swear
Don't see why I should share
But you don't seem to care
I'm drowning in despair
This is my worst nightmare
Is he handsome and debonair?
Is he the answer to your prayer?
Does he have a full head of hair
Or are you dazzled from the sun's glare?
Does he dance like Fred Astaire?
Does he use mugs or chinaware?
Does he apply Ambre Solaire?
Have you ever seen him bare?
How does he compare?
Is your sex life rare?
You say you met him where?
Is he in a wheelchair?
Did his sight suddenly impair?
Can he still climb a stair?
I need some fresh air
While you my tea prepare
I'm not upset, au contraire
I'll get myself an au pair
Not stay in with Solitaire.

Andy MacDonald

COLOURS

My name is *Pain*
My colour is orange
Veins of flowing fluid,
Deep slopes of sharpness
In the cavities of time
Pressing against your organs,
Extracting bitter tears,
Contracting your heart.

My name is *Hope*
My colour is yellow
Wires of metallic nets,
Needles of faith,
Spread around you
Like thin rays of thunder
Conducting electricity,
Empowering your mind.

My name is *Love*
My colour is red
Vivid drops of tender ruby
Poured over your skin,
Showers of ink and paint,
Dominated by shadows
In the light of antic flames
Burning your heart,
Caressing your soul.

My name is Strength
My colour is *love*
Shades of acceptance,
Bright nuances of light,
Depth of belief,
Brushes of inspiration,
Dipped in beauty
Painting the canvas of life!

Laura LME

POETRY AND I

Poetry and I
Like vision in my eyes
Peace of my mind
Love from the kind
Pure like rivers flow
Beautiful like roses grow
It makes me forget love's pain
Anger that travels my vein
Poetry and I
Like constellation in the sky
To beautify the night
Which brings in darkness, some light
It's the palette of art
Awakening emotion in my heart
It's like the fragrance
I'm the essence
Poetry and I
One world to form beauty
Exhilaration and creativity
Serenity around with appreciation
It's my very great passion
Like sea and shore
Words and thoughts
From what we learned and taught
Poetry, my bosom friend
Like pen in my hand
Scribbling day, night
Like the heart and beat cling so tight
Forming a rhythm of life
My intellect like a barrel of ideas
With complete attention to make it not a lie
Alive like when you read it
The bulb of your mind would be lit
Like words popping out the white sheet
Fluctuating in the air
Bringing you along with the theme
When I see water flows and falls
It brings me to springs and waterfalls
Like my soul and heart couple on
As in a strong bond
Poetry and I.

Shazia Ameerun

FANFARE

It doesn't cost much so I can't complain
And I will be glad to arrive
Courtesy of Ryanair,
Despite smug self-congratulation.
It's been two hours in cramped space
I was tricked by ambiguous info
On the booking page re luggage
So I'm carrying one case
Having paid for two.
£70! However we did not crash!
Though that thought provokes
A darker contemplation.
Had we crashed
(On the optimistic assumption
of my arrival at the Pearly Gates).
Which would be worst?
Hearing Gabriel's trumpet fanfare
Or St Peter's dry reflection
'Another group from Ryanair
Arrives ahead of schedule!'

Mike Richardson

LIVE YOUR DREAMS

Live your dreams to fulfil your purpose,
If your dreams die you are lost like the wind in
The humming rains.
Your life is just like the sunset sinking in the west,
I see you today but tomorrow your soul
Takes a quiet rest in death.
Live out your dreams and aspirations before you die;
You are a blooming rose smiling in the garden of life;
Then a sudden wind comes and blows you away
Like smoke into the clouds.
Live your dreams to reach your goals,
If your dreams die your purpose in life is like a ship
Sinking into the river of your heart.
When all our work on Earth is done,
And we realise it's time for us to say goodbye;
Then we shall turn the keys from our mortal doors
And only our dreams will live on after we are gone.
You must not live with a dream but live with
An immortal dream to change the world;
If your dreams die you are just dust
And shadows fluttering in the voyage of the eternal wind.

Gideon Cecil

NOTHING TO WORRY ABOUT

One day copies another
In the looking-glass
Of the wallpapered bedroom
With dead anecdotes

I am not looking, but . . .
I can see the lagoon
From the bay window
Of my cushioned window sill

I am not listening, but . . .
I can hear inside the house
Of burning words
Shut in loud questions

I am not touching, but . . .
I can feel rising hedges
In a surfing game
Over the fields of grey

I am not close, but . . .
I can smell the sweat of pain
Rising like arched fog
Tanned in seawater

I am not eating, but . . .
I can taste what has been lost
From that dream in the pillows
Against crimson rolling tongues

One shape copies another
In the paralysed glass
Of fading unshaped voices
No new beginning . . . no new end.

Mariana Zavati Gadner

A RUSSIAN DREAM

Through the snow-covered streets of Moscow
Through the lone and lovely villages
Of the vast Russian valleys
Through the leaf-shed woods
Of the snow-covered Siberian mountains.
I will walk . . .
And your face will make me nostalgic.

In the mornings of St Petersburg and Moscow
In the haunting nights
Through the deserted lanes of Bilibino
I will walk . . .
And your memories will flatter my mind.

While crossing the River Don
And while chatting with the Cossacks
I surely remember you
Because . . .
Once I loved you.

Vishnu Sivaram Nair

POISED TO LIVE

A rebirth is near
Life is due to start
She's poised to utter
With urges, actions and lessons
Of freedom and exuberance
For breaking a silent death.

A pathway is stopped
Death is redefined
She's poised to create
With sightlines, crossroads and starlights
At mirror and mirage edges
To make silent miracles.

A reform is on
Miracles are apt
She's poised to scribble
With letters, numbers and patterns
On everlasting game play cards
Thus ending a silent life.

Eunice Ogunkoya

GOD SHOWED ME

I trusted in myself until the day came,
I don't want fame.
I am not like the others,
I go to the park to be alone,
I am what I am.

These kids came one day,
They laughed at me,
They shouted at me,
But God showed me.

I felt sad inside,
But I didn't show it on the outside,
I just let them do it,
They tormented me bit by bit,
But God showed me.

God is by my side through thick and thin,
They stopped at last,
It's all in the past now,
But every day from then on I've looked
Through the window for them.

God is there somewhere and I'm waiting
For Him.

Daniel Whitehouse

UNTITLED

As we dance on the floor
My body is there
For you to explore
And you're fully aware.

I'm the girl of your dreams
Or so you think
Because that's how it seems –
Your vision in pink.

You're in for a surprise
When you take me home
You'll find it's all lies
I'm spoiled to the bone.

I'm filled with fatigue
I'm deeply depressed
You'll lose your intrigue
When you see my breast

I was robbed of my pride
When cancer arrived
My entire body has died
And yet my mind survives.

Jessica Tomlin

FOR YOU
(For my friend, Hannah)

Here's a little poem
I wrote especially for you
In case you've wondered
Or ever feel blue

You're always on my mind
No matter the time of day
And you're the star of my dreams
You chased the others away

You've changed my way of thinking
Into something good
And everything that I didn't understand
I now understood

You make me want to be better
Be someone who stands tall
Who's not afraid to try new things
And not scared to fall

You are beautiful and perfect
You knock me off my feet
And you make me fall in love with you
Most times when we meet.

Chloe Catlin

STRANGE ANNEX

Footsteps lay a silent soul on a
Path that won't be touched. Oxygen
Tastes so plain, yet hunger begs
For more.

I'm a moving target within a safe zone
Walking into a life full of nothing,
Passing rooms filled with falcons to
Their prey.

Ghosts seem to be my only company
Taking it easy . . . it will all be fine. So
Lonely, yet I still hear you. Each step I take
Fades into history – without you.

I see the end, but no future in sight
Where are you? Your presence is
So cold to the bone, but your memory
Is still locked to the brain.

Eye to eye – nothing but pain.
Exchanging weapons for hearts – I'm
Coming for you. I shall reach out to you . . .
Before the distance meets you first.

Stephanie Caldwell

DREAMS

Where did the ghosts of yesterday go?
Ripping out our souls
Bearing down on spirits – that once were whole.
Should we travel down that road,
Or in the present stay?
But what about our future –
Which is yesterday today.
Can you hear them calling –
Telling you what to do?
Can you hear the inner voice –
Calming you?
Am I really dreaming?
Sometimes it seems so real –
Then I wake and know what I can really feel

Similar to a snowflake which has drifted far away
And melted on a grain of sand –
That's where it will stay.
But dreams are made of many things –
Some do come true –
And if every one of us can help each other –
That's what we should do –
We come into the world with nothing
We leave with just our name
But in-between if we have cared –
Life hasn't been in vain,
So just keep on dreaming –
You will never know–
The signs are there for you to see –
Trust your instinct –
Let it be.

Marje M Armstrong

NO NAME

(For Ocean)

Amniotic warm floating in space
Your hands cover up your tiny face

Veins show like roads, a tiny beating heart
This is just the beginning at the very start

Tiny legs curled up as if to keep you warm
All detailing superb, a miraculous form

Umbilical cord feeds your brain,
Capillaries, flesh, muscle and vein

Eyelids are present in the shapes of folds
Very young indeed, at five months old.

The head is developed, tiny nails grow
Life is moving, deep in her stow

Lips are completed and round little nose
Embryo you have a distinctive pose

Moving now you jerk and swim
Even hair on your head, is trim

About the size of a young child's shoe
Your delicate skin, a transparent hue

So fragile and dependent, working on growth
Everything is normal, you have both

Little spaceman floating, no light and no air
So much concern, you haven't a care.

Mama gasps, a fist smoothing under her skin
A moment so glorious, so special, a win.

Meia Allegranza

TECHNOLOGY

Technology just grows and grows
Where will it end? Well, no one knows
From busy factories employing many hands
Now just a robot in a far-off land.
After pushing the buttons you are none the wiser
And Mr Robot cannot answer you either.
How do you ask what you want to know
When a cold piece of metal is programmed so?
Please bring back the people who were friendly and kind
Willing to help on the end of the line.
Fill up our factories with a workforce whose skill
Is wasted in looking for a job they can fill.

Children cannot read, well that's no surprise
Just look at text spelling to see reason why.
You think I'm old fashioned to read a good book
Talk to a person, who bothers to look.
'How do you know that?' my grandchildren ask
Because when I studied, the knowledge was to last.
Not run off on the computer that just rushes past.

Audrey A Allocca

A NAME SHAPES A CHILD'S DESTINY

Charlie Toogood . . .
On detention at school again
'I hate my name,' he muttered to himself.
The other children never let him
Forget his surname.
'Why can't I be called anything
Other than Toogood?'
'I don't like everyone sniggering
Every time my name is spoken by a teacher.'
'I wanna be a Smith or White.'
'Toogoody, goody, goody, goody
Too bloody good two shoes!'
Charlie clenched his teeth and his fists
And cried by himself
At the cruel jibes and taunts
That played round and round his head.
From now on he shouted
'I am going to become Charlie, really bad!'

Yazmin White

THE DARKENED ROOM

A shadow from the window above
Time a reflection across the dust and cobwebs
A clock stopped at half-nine
Hear the rain across the cracked windowpane
The house of cards amidst the breeze
A candle does flicker of travesty
The chair in the corner, a bone-chilling freeze
The paintings sit for all to see
The darkness, the silence of the hall
The smell of damp of Victorian decline
The smell of bones entwined
A dance where phantoms dare
A flicker of candlelight going up the stair
The light through the shadowy doorway
A canvas that only weeps
A floorboard that merely creaks,
A draught from the fireplace, unlit for centuries
A light so barren, a crack under the door
A face, a gasp at the window
Winter, a storm, amidst the snow
A room of apparitions, we sit at the table
Our wedding feast, our horse in the stable
The music plays our tune once more
Our honeymoon, travel to distant shore
Outward to be a fool, to die alone as not a tool
That ours is not the windswept rainy night
The lines across the countryside.
Where lovers fall, where love has died,
That ours could be as ghost in flight.
I sat, a bridge of content
Watching ripples form, a reflection of your face.
I sat, the solemn hearse in sight
In the water to sink without trace.

Barry Powell

FORWARD POETRY INFORMATION

We hope you have enjoyed reading this book - and that you will continue to enjoy it in the coming years.

If you like reading and writing poetry drop us a line, or give us a call, and we'll send you a free information pack.

Alternatively if you would like to order further copies of this book or any of our other titles, then please give us a call or log onto our website at www.forwardpoetry.co.uk.

Forward Poetry Information
Remus House
Coltsfoot Drive
Peterborough
PE2 9BF
(01733) 890099